N.N. SHNEIDMAN is Professor of Russian at Erindale College in the University of Toronto.

Although considerable attention has been given to dissident Soviet writers who have been exiled or driven underground, the officially published works of Soviet writers are almost unknown in the West. This book concentrates on those writers who have produced works of considerable interest and merit despite editorial controls.

The opening chapter examines recent trends and the relationship between literary theory and practice, particularly in the light of the broadening horizons of official 'socialist realism.' Shneidman traces the creative development of six of the most gifted and popular Russian prose writers of the decade, emphasizing their publications of the 1970s and their diverse themes and styles. Sergei Zalygin sets his work in the revolutionary past. Vasil' Bykov and Iurii Bondarev write on war themes. Iurii Trifonov depicts the ordinary life of the city intelligentsia. Valentin Rasputin's stories are concerned with the fate of the Siberian peasant. Chingiz Aitmatov deals with problems of universal significance in a Kirghiz setting.

This book recognizes the difficulties faced by contemporary creative writers in the USSR, and reflects the intellectual, ideological, and political atmosphere in which they work.

N.N. SHNEIDMAN

Soviet Literature
in the 1970s:
Artistic diversity and
ideological conformity

UNIVERSITY OF TORONTO PRESS

Toronto Buffalo London

© University of Toronto Press 1979
Toronto Buffalo London
Printed in Canada

Library of Congress Cataloging in Publication Data

Shneidman, NN
    Soviet literature in the 1970s.

    Bibliography: p.
    Includes index.
    1. Russian fiction – 20th century – History and criticism. I. Title.
    PG3098.4.S48   891.7'09'0044   79-14942
    ISBN 0-8020-5463-3

Contents

Preface

Literature is a dynamic phenomenon which finds itself in constant change. Each work throws a new light on the artistic evolution of its author and adjusts our perception of his creative activity. A thorough understanding of the Soviet literary scene requires a familiarity with Soviet life in general and the social, economic, ideological, and political forces which stimulate the development of Soviet society. This investigation of artistic and social problems is conducted, therefore, in a combined and integrated manner, an approach which should enable the Western reader to understand better the works of today's Soviet authors, and Soviet society in general.

I rely in this study mainly on original sources, and all translations from Russian in the text, unless quoted from English sources, are my own. Any transliteration system from one language into another is arbitrary; I have adopted here the widely used transliteration system of the Library of Congress. Titles, when they appear for the first time in the text, are given in Russian with an English translation in parentheses. The same titles later appear only in Russian.

I would like to acknowledge my debt and express my gratitude to all those who helped me in the course of my work on this book. I am indebted to Professors K. Lantz and G.S.N. Luckyj, and Mr J. Winter, who have read parts of the manuscript and offered constructive criticism. A special note of thanks is due to the Soviet scholars and writers whom I had an opportunity to interview on my recent visits to the USSR. Needless to say, my discussions with them helped me to gain a better understanding of the intricate forces which determine the evolution of Soviet prose.

I gratefully acknowledge the permission of the editors of *Canadian Slavonic Papers* and the *Russian Language Journal* to use material previously published in those journals. Sections of several chapters of this book have appeared there in slightly different form.

This book has been published with the help of grants from the Canadian Federation for the Humanities, using funds provided by the Social Sciences and Humanities Research Council of Canada, and from the Publications Fund of University of Toronto Press; this assistance is greatly appreciated.

I acknowledge with pleasure the assistance of different institutions and the help and advice of my colleagues and friends, but I accept sole responsibility for any inaccuracies and mistakes that may exist in this book.

Toronto, Canada   N.N.S.

Introduction

One of the main characteristics of the development of Soviet literature in the 1970s is a polarization between the literature officially published by Soviet citizens in the USSR and the so-called 'dissident' literature, published within the Soviet Union as well as in the West.

The post-Stalin 'thaws' resulted in a certain relaxation of literary controls, and a number of writers began to deal in their works with controversial problems, frequently offering solutions unacceptable to the new Soviet leadership. The desire of the party and of the Soviet government to streamline the development of literature resulted in the application of new pressures on writers to create works of art conforming with the present-day objectives of the Soviet state. This new pressure on the artist, applied with increasing intensity since the early 1960s, has led in turn to a clear split in Soviet literature, with one group of able writers acquiescing in the literary policies of the party and joining the official camp, and the other group being driven underground.

As recently as in the late 1960s it was often difficult to make a clear distinction between 'official' and 'dissident' writers. Some writers were publishing simultaneously in official Soviet journals and in *samizdat* and *tamizdat* publications.* During the 1970s, these two trends in Soviet literature have been re-emphasized, with 'dissident' writers being driven deeper underground and, in many cases, exiled. Thus, for example, a number of prominent Soviet writers, including Aleksandr

---

Samizdat refers to literature unofficially published and clandestinely circulated in the Soviet Union, usually reproduced by hand, typewriter, or mimeograph. The term *tamizdat* has several interpretations. Most commonly it refers to works by Soviet authors unapproved for official publication in the USSR and published abroad. Some, however, include in *tamizdat* only works by émigré authors, and consider works by Soviet writers, barred from official publication in the USSR and published in the West, as belonging to *samizdat* literature.

Solzhenitsyn, Viktor Nekrasov, Vladimir Maksimov, Andrei Siniavskii, reside now in the West, while others like Vladimir Voinovich and Vladimir Kornilov have been expelled from the Writers Union and deprived from earning a livelihood in the Soviet Union. They continue to write and endeavour to have their works published in the West.

This study of Soviet literature of the seventies has been prompted by a desire to adjust the imbalance between the treatment in the West of Soviet official literature and of 'dissident' literature and it deals, therefore, only with works appearing in Soviet official publications, and written by members of the Soviet Union of Writers. The Soviets often complain, with some justification, that exaggerated attention is devoted in the West to 'dissident' writers, regardless of the artistic quality of their works, and usually at the expense of the literature officially published in the USSR. Indeed, Russian literature officially published in the Soviet Union receives inadequate attention in the West. Few Soviet titles are translated into English and Western literary scholars and critics are often late in summarizing and discussing the most recent developments on the Soviet literary scene. In addition, studies of Soviet literature appearing in the West often fail to make a clear distinction between writers who reside in the Soviet Union and who, at least publicly, adhere to the tenets of the party; and those who have rejected the policies of the Soviet state and publish mainly in *samizdat* and *tamizdat* publications.

Thus, for example, the second edition of Marc Slonim's history of Soviet literature, *Soviet Russian Literature. Writers and Problems 1917–1977* (New York 1977), devotes little attention to the best contemporary Soviet writers. The names of Chingiz Aitmatov, Sergei Zalygin, Vasil' Bykov, Iurii Bondarev, are hardly mentioned. The most space is devoted to writers such as Maksimov or Siniavskii, who are now for all practical purposes Russian émigré writers.

More important by far is the recently published monograph *Soviet Russian Literature Since Stalin* (Cambridge 1978) by Deming Brown. Professor Brown discusses in his book the development of unofficial Soviet literature and devotes separate chapters to the creative work of Solzhenitsyn and Siniavskii. Yet he also makes a thorough investigation and analysis of the evolution of official Soviet literature in the fifties and sixties, and he discusses at some length the creative work of the most important of today's Soviet writers and poets. Although Professor Brown's conclusions are, with few exceptions, based on his discussion of works of the fifties and sixties, they are relevant to the situation of more recent Soviet prose.

It is unnecessary to say that with few exceptions the level of official Soviet prose, and in particular of the Soviet novel which appears to be at an impasse, does not come up to the general expectations of the early sixties. Nevertheless, the study of current Soviet literature is important because literature often reflects in many ways the intellectual, ideological, and political atmosphere of the country. Furthermore, the literature appearing in the 1970s, more than that appearing at any other time, could be regarded as a reflection of Soviet reality.

There are presently close to 8000 members of the Soviet Union of Writers. This number includes writers, poets, critics, translators, writing in seventy-six different languages. And yet, when we speak of Soviet literature proper, we refer to the small number of Soviet writers who transcend all national and territorial boundaries; those whose works are published in the leading Soviet Russian literary journals, regardless of the language in which they have been originally written. There are few non-Russian writers who gain nation-wide prominence, but those who do become increasingly identified with Soviet literature in general and with the Russian language in particular – often at the expense of their national cultures.

The bulk of creative literature appearing in the Soviet Union, receives no mention in official Soviet literary criticism. Most of the books published by local, regional, and republic publishing houses are stored on the shelves of libraries and bookstores with the readers showing little interest in them. At the same time, works by better Soviet writers such as Aitmatov, Valentin Rasputin, or Iurii Trifonov are impossible to obtain; the moment they appear, they are sold out, in many instances, 'under the counter.' The leaders of the Soviet literary establishment decry the fact that the appearance of most Soviet works of literature passes unnoticed. As one critic complained: 'nine tenths of all works of literature published receive no critical attention whatsoever.'[1] One can only surmise that many of these works are mediocre and uninspiring, written by writers without gift or calling.

Literary criticism should be playing an important role in the development of literature in the Soviet Union. However, instead of helping to detect and promote young gifted writers, official critics more often hamper and discourage the natural development of innate talent. Such forceful intrusion into the evolution of talent, by its very nature individual and resenting outside interference, is fraught with serious consequences for the future of Soviet literature.

It is possible even to say that the gifted young writer has almost completely disappeared from the Soviet literary scene. It is well known that in the nineteenth century Fedor Dostoevskii, Leo Tolstoi, and Nikolai Gogol' produced brilliant work while still in their early twenties. Even in the early Soviet days writers such as Konstantin Fedin, Leonid Leonov, or Aleksandr Fadeev created many of their best works while still in their twenties. Now 'a young Soviet prose writer is not so young any-more; he is well over thirty,'[2] and usually has higher or secondary specialized technical education. Thus it seems that young people in Russia with an innate gift for writing and creating imaginative literature have disappeared; or, at least, they are hiding somewhere under the surface. The fact that many aspiring authors study in literary institutes or attend special courses for creative writers before being admitted to the Writers Union is of little help in lowering the average age of Soviet writers. One can only presume that censorship, official criticism, and editorial control have something to do with this situation.

Good and controversial literature appearing in the Soviet Union is immediately recognized by the reading public. Such works are in great demand and are sold out overnight; their authors gain instant popularity. There is little that can be done nowadays to a writer, even if his works are severely criticized, provided the works appear in official Soviet publications and have been passed by the editors and censors.

By contrast, the position of the editor of a journal is very vulnerable, and he is always exposed to danger. There are today few editors of the stature of Aleksandr Tvardovskii, ready to stand up for what they believe in and defend real talent. Most editors play it safe. Indeed, they hamper the evolution of real talent by avoiding originality, changing style, and using a number of other means to emasculate the main idea of a work of art and remove the individuality of the writer from the work he has created. Many writers are forced to submit to such treatment because writing is their only means of earning a livelihood; others are sent to school to learn *how* to write if they want to be published.

The relationship of an author with his editor is well depicted in a recent novelette by Liliia Beliaeva, appearing in the 1976 volume of *Novyi mir* (New World). The writer in question replies to the demands of the editor and says: 'I understand you well. For you the whole question is about four unnecessary paragraphs. For me it means the loss of an idea. The loss of the truth; of a very essential part of it.'[3] The editor continues to insist and the writer requests the return of his manuscript. The hero of the story is one of the few who are ready to sacrifice their material well-being and to stand up for what they believe in. In real life, however, most writers have no choice but to submit.

Despite all these difficulties, a number of Soviet writers do manage to bypass the hurdles of editorial control and create works of art of considerable merit. Some of these writers are themselves literary bureaucrats in high positions. Others try to avoid controversial problems of ideology and politics and concentrate instead on the study of man.

Current Soviet literature is a huge subject, and it would be futile to try to give a full picture of it in an investigation of limited scope. I will endeavour to draw a general picture of the most important aspects of the evolution of Soviet literature in the last decade, with particular emphasis on the relationship between the theory of literature and literary practice. I will deal mainly with Russian prose. Works by non-Russian authors which transcend national confines in their thematic and artistic importance are also included; but only if they are written in, or translated into, Russian.

Chapter one gives a general survey of the Soviet literary scene today. I explore in this chapter the general pattern of literary evolution in the Soviet Union in the last decade. In chapters two to six I discuss the creative work of Chingiz Aitmatov, Iurii Bondarev, Vasil' Bykov, Valentin Rasputin, Iurii Trifonov, and Sergei Zalygin – the most gifted, prominent, and popular Soviet writers of the 1970s. Three of them were awarded the 1977 Soviet State Prize for literature: Rasputin for his novelette 'Zhivi i pomni' (Live and Remember), Bondarev for his novel *Bereg* (The Shore), and Aitmatov for the screen version of his story 'Belyi parokhod' (The White Steamship).[4] While I analyse in these chapters the whole creative path of the writers discussed, the emphasis is on the most recent evolution of their creative talents and on the works published in the 1970s.

There are a number of significant contemporary Soviet writers such as, for example, Iurii Nagibin, Andrei Bitov, Vil' Lipatov, and others who, due to the limitation of space, do not receive any mention in this study. The object of this investigation, however, is not to discuss the works of all Soviet writers, but to give a general picture of the Soviet literary scene. The writers selected for detailed discussion are those who stand out most prominently above the general level of Soviet literature, and each of them represents a different trend in Soviet literature. Thus, Zalygin deals mainly with the investigation of the revolutionary past of the young Soviet state. Bykov and Bondarev devote most of their time to the theme of war. Trifonov depicts the *byt* (everyday life) of the city intelligentsia. Rasputin's stories are concerned with the fate of the Siberian peasant, while Aitmatov deals with problems of universal significance in a Kirghiz setting.

I hope that this study will be of interest to the student of Russian literature and of Soviet society, and that it will stimulate a better understanding of the intricate forces which guide the creative process of writers in the Soviet Union.

SOVIET LITERATURE IN THE 1970s

1 ❧ The Soviet Literary Scene

Soviet literature is a complex multidimensional phenomenon. It can be examined not only as an aesthetic but as a sociological phenomenon having broad cultural, national, and ideological implications. Soviet literature is different from Russian pre-revolutionary and Western literatures primarily by being a vehicle of ideology; it reflects in part the author's personal view of natural and social phenomena, but is also required to deliver a specific message. The new realities of life and the changing objectives of the post-Stalin Soviet state have influenced the development of literature and the arts in the Soviet Union. But regardless of this evolution, Soviet literary theory is based on the general ideological premises of the Communist Party. This literary theory is supposed, officially at least, to permeate every aspect of artistic activity and should guide Soviet writers in their creative endeavours.

THEORETICAL PERSPECTIVES

It is well known that in the days of Stalin socialist realism was the official 'method' of Soviet literature. The official formulation of socialist realism, adopted in 1934 by the First Congress of Soviet Writers, 'requires from the artist a truthful, historically concrete representation of reality in its revolutionary development. Moreover, truth and historical completeness of artistic representation must be combined with the task of ideological transformation and education of the working man in the spirit of socialism.' There is no need to elaborate here in detail the specific prerequisites of socialist realism or their practical application to the creative work of Soviet writers. Any history of Soviet literature of the Stalin period, regardless of its place of publication, will supply this information.

It is well known that the enforced implementation of the rigid principles of socialist realism – which limited the stylistic range of a writer and required that a didactic message be delivered in a work of art – stifled the development of Soviet literature and drove many gifted writers into oblivion. In the days of Stalin, particularly beginning with the middle of the 1930s, literary policy was implemented by force. Works of dubious value to the Soviet state had little chance of eluding the vigilant eye of the censor. Writers who dared to challenge the system were regarded not only as deviating artists but also as ideological adversaries, and were usually faced with appropriate consequences.

The situation changed after the death of Stalin and, in particular, after the Twentieth Party Congress at which the 'personality cult' of Stalin was denounced. A number of writers liberated from the dangers of Stalinist repression began to turn out works in which they presented a picture of reality contrary to the criteria established for the literature of socialist realism. But since there has been no official rejection of the old theoretical premises of Soviet literature, and since socialist realism continues to be the 'official method' approved by the Party, a disparity has developed between the theoretical premises of literature and their practical implementation. On the one hand, Soviet leaders persist in maintaining that socialist realism should remain the guiding norm of Soviet literature; on the other hand, they do not prevent writers and theoreticians from discussing and examining what socialist realism actually means, and how it should be implemented.

This new development in Soviet literature is by no means a painless process, because there are few literary scholars or critics who could agree on what the term socialist realism actually means, and on how it should be applied. In the days of Stalin the life of literary scholars appeared to be less complicated because everyone knew how 'good' literature was to be written and what socialist realism was all about. Now everyone proclaims that socialist realism continues indeed to be the basic method of Soviet literature, yet no one is able to define properly its meaning.

In the Soviet Union today literature, instead of following theoretical guidelines, develops (to a degree) in a spontaneous manner. Thus, theoreticians and literary scholars are forced to react to literary practice by adapting theory to the realities of the literary scene. Writers strive for creative freedom. Literary scholars and critics, who are often members of editorial boards of literary journals and publishing houses, and thus the guardians of ideological purity, endeavour to 'streamline' the creative activity of writers, leading them in the required direction. It appears that Soviet literary scholars have now lost much of the power they held in the days of Stalin and they can no longer prescribe how 'good' literature is to be written. By turning into active literary critics, theorists of literature endeavour to influence the literary process in two ways: firstly, by shaping public opinion; secondly, by forcing the writers to create works of literature which would best serve the ideological and political objectives of the Communist Party and the Soviet state.

The new relationship of theory and practice in post-Stalin Soviet literature has generated a heated discussion on the very essence of Soviet literary theory in general and of socialist realism in particular. The debate, which has continued with undiminishing intensity throughout the 1960s and '70s, has produced a number of divergent views. The debate concerns itself primarily with the relationship of socialist realism to Soviet and socialist art in general, and to the question of whether the term 'socialist realism' is synonymous with the term 'socialist art' or 'Soviet art.'

Some theoreticians, including the notable scholar V.R. Shcherbina, see no distinction between the art of socialist realism and socialist art in general; they suggest that socialist realism embraces the works of all socialist writers, including those of Valerii Briusov, Aleksandr Blok, Sergei Esenin, and Boris Pasternak.[1] Others vehemently oppose such suppositions, and claim that the 'application of the concept of "socialist realism" to the works of these writers can produce only extreme amazement.'[2] So far this continuous dialogue has produced few results because the suggested definitions of particular theoretical notions and terms lack clarity; the interpretation of the same theoretical concepts by different scholars leads to completely different conclusions. Moreover, leading Soviet literary scholars excel in their efforts to criticize and repudiate the views of their colleagues and opponents, without being able themselves to define 'socialist realism' in a way that would satisfy all, and which could be accepted as an official guideline for contemporary Soviet literature.

In the days of Stalin socialist realism and its prerequisites were clearly defined, and only literature conforming with the accepted requirements could appear in print. In present conditions it is sometimes difficult to determine whether or not a certain work by a Soviet writer, who is a member of the Writers Union, conforms with the requirements of socialist realism. One Soviet theoretician even suggests that Soviet literary scholarship is presently at the crossroads, facing two choices. 'The first possibility is to adhere to the initial interpretation of socialist realism, which would require, however, a sharp limitation in the number of works included among those complying with its requirements. In this case let us suppose that *Neterpenie* [Impatience] by Iurii Trifonov and *Solenaia Pad'* [Salt Valley] by Sergei Zalygin would be considered as works of socialist realism (i.e. epic), as opposed to such works as 'Obmen' [The Exchange] and *Iuzhno-Amerikanskii Variant* [South-American Variant] by the same writers. The second possibility is to develop a deeper theoretical conception of socialist realism which could encompass a variety of works representing different types of literature.'[3] Indeed, Soviet literary scholarship has found itself for over two decades at the crossroads, unable to make a definite choice. Such a situation would have been unthinkable in the days of Stalin.

The existing disparity between the theory and practice of Soviet literature and the search for a consensus in the understanding and interpretation of literary theory have generated a number of extreme views on the essence of socialist realism and its relationship to art in general. The leading Soviet literary theoretician, D. Markov, tries to sum up the dialogue by suggesting that three different opinions have been expressed on the subject. One point of view adheres to the application of a number of inflexible narrow dogmatic rules and criteria to the interpretation of a work of art – an approach which, according to Markov, should be regarded as a dogmatic bastardization of socialist realism. Another extreme view advocates the abolition of all boundaries, giving the writer complete artistic freedom in depicting reality. However, some claim that such an approach would lead to the removal of the ideological foundations of socialist art. Markov himself suggests a third path, one which rejects both approaches related above and which 'regards socialist realism as an essentially new aesthetic system which rejects both extremely narrow and dogmatic norms, and the removal and undermining of the ideological foundations of socialist art.'[4]

It thus appears that Markov assumes a middle of the road position, suggesting that while there is a danger in exposing a writer's creative work to the application of a set of narrow dogmatic rules, the ideological essence and educational value of Soviet literature must be retained at any cost. L. Iakimenko suggests that socialist realism should be presently regarded as 'an essentially new aesthetic formation which most fully expresses the ideological unity and stylistic diversity of Soviet art'; and that the dialogue on the very essence of socialist realism 'has been presently transformed into a discussion about artistic forms, or more precisely, about the forms of "artistic generalization" which characterize socialist realism as a creative method.'[5]

It is well known that in the thirties and forties the literature of socialist realism adhered to conventional literary forms. It was against unnecessary experimentation, against modernism and pure aestheticism in art, and against the introduction of artistic forms which could distract the reader from the socially important content and the ideological message delivered by the author. Now, it is asserted that 'socialist realism (as any realism in general) does not adhere to any particular forms.'[6] 'Neither "forms of real life" nor the romantic or conditional forms, fantasy, grotesque, or different kinds of deformations are contradictory to the method of socialist realism if they assist the writer in the re-creation of a deeper, more subtle, and correct picture of reality which is in the process of continuous and complex transformation.'[7]

It is even suggested that socialist realism is an 'open aesthetic system with broad possibilities and a variety of different forms for the perception and artistic re-creation of reality'; however, one should have in mind 'an openness which has evolved aesthetically as a result of the consistent application of a Marxist-Leninist world-outlook,' and that 'there is nothing farther from the truth than to presume that the openness of the aesthetics of socialist realism means a convergence with modernist trends.'[8] It appears thus that an artist is granted complete freedom in selecting any artistic form, style, or method of artistic presentation suitable for his art – provided it assists in delivering an artistic message which best serves the general objectives of Soviet literature.

Similarly, a new approach has been suggested for the treatment of the positive hero in Soviet literature. In the classical literature of socialist realism the positive hero had to be at the heart of a work of art. In most cases he was the main protagonist whose actions were to be followed and emulated by the readers. All this has apparently changed. T. Motyleva writes in *Voprosy literatury* (Problems of Literature) that 'the art of socialist realism can fulfil its educational objectives in different ways. The meaning of heroic characters and their effect which enobles and spiritually elevates the reader is exceedingly important. Art, however, can influence the minds and hearts of the people not only with the help of the positive but also with the help of negative examples, thus heightening the ethical vigilance of the reader to the types and views which are alien to socialism.'[9]

In the past, writers of socialist realism usually supplied the solutions to problems posed in their works. There was little doubt with whom the author identified and on whose side his sympathies were. Since many readers are now more sophisticated than their counterparts of the thirties and forties, straightforward didacticism is discouraged because it may have an adverse effect on the reading public. In line with the above, T. Motyleva suggests that 'socialist realism does not in the least require that the author should state his position in a declarative form. In a political poem or in a novel depicting sharp class conflicts, the blunt expression of the author's views is natural and necessary; but in works such as love lyrics, in a psychological tale, or in literature describing the so-called *byt* such forms may be out of place.'[10]

This modified interpretation of the prerequisites of socialist realism makes it possible to include within the canon a number of current works of literature which lack a positive hero or a positive message. There are, for example, few positive heroes in the recent works of one of the most gifted of today's Soviet writers, Chingiz Aitmatov. On the contrary, 'evil' is victorious in many of his stories. Official representatives of the state and the Party, who abuse their power and needlessly humiliate others, go unpunished. Law-breakers are on the loose.

It seems, however, that it is possible to place the works of Aitmatov within the confines of socialist realism because they have educational value along with artistic merit. The intensity of narration, which is characteristic of Aitmatov's art, and the tragic quality of the situations presented by the writer excite the reader. They make him hate the 'evil-doers'; they provoke his indignation and animosity towards the negative protagonists and they incite him to fight against such people in daily Soviet life. This does not mean, however, that such works are received with unanimous approval by all. Many Soviet readers and critics continue to demand that an unequivocal message be present in a work of art and that there should be no ambiguity in the position of the protagonists or in the author's relationship to his heroes.

All this having been said, the question remains: what is the definition of socialist realism today? In the past, Soviet theory of literature, which aspired to become an exact science, usually supplied precise definitions for theoretical rules and notions. It appears that now all this has changed. The noted Soviet scholar Iu. Barabash even suggests, in *Novyi mir*, that the 'contemporary scholar of the humanities is torn apart by contradictions,' and that the application of the notion of exactitude to the humanities is not synonymous with its application to the sciences.[11] And yet Soviet literary scholarship finds itself in a paradoxical situation. On the one hand, few writers and critics would disagree that changes in the old formulation of socialist realism are timely and necessary; on the other hand, the new definitions of this term proposed by different scholars are so general, vague, and incoherent that they can in no way serve as a guide for the writer who wishes to comply with its requirements.

Even conservative Soviet scholars, such as A. Metchenko, A. Dubrovin, and L. Lazarev, admit that the old theoretical premises of socialist literature, developed in the early thirties, have outlived their usefulness. They agree that changes are necessary but they are uncertain about the nature of the changes required.[12] They warn of the danger of a policy of strict regulations for literature but they assert also that 'the art of socialist realism has its boundaries ... not iron hoops, not webs or pressing walls, but boundaries.'[13] However, instead of specifying clearly where these boundaries are to be sought, the same scholars resort to the old cliché according to which the essence of socialist realism should be expressed in its ideological unity and artistic diversity. For all practical purposes most literary theoreticians view the dialogue on the all-round development of the principle of socialist realism as 'a struggle for the victory of socialist ideals and norms of life; an ideological struggle in which there could be no compromises.'[14] It follows from the above that one can write today about anything in the Soviet Union as long as one does not challenge openly the foundations of Soviet society and does not question the policies of the Soviet state.

Among the numerous, often overlapping, formulations of the term 'socialist realism' in circulation in the Soviet Union, it is worthwhile to single out the one proposed by S.M. Petrov. He suggests that 'socialist realism is realistic art which reflects the experience of man's struggle for the victory of socialism. It is based on the world-outlook of scientific socialism and it promotes the advancement of mankind from capitalism to socialism and communism, as well as the education of a new harmoniously developed man.'[15] This and other similar definitions of socialist realism are usually supplemented by a number of guiding concepts which the writers of socialist realism are to follow.

A. Metchenko propounds that 'the main principles of socialist realism, which have been tested in the struggle for the socialist transformation of the world, are truthfulness to life, communist *partiinost'* [party principles and spirit], and the *narodnost'* [national spirit] of art.'[16] The term *narodnost'* became a popular part of Soviet literary terminology in the second half of the 1930s, in the period of the struggle against vulgar 'sociologism' in art which overemphasized the application of the principle of *klassovost'* [class character] in the interpretation of artistic values.[17] It is considered now that a work of literature complies with the requirements of *narodnost'* if it is written in a manner accessible to the masses and can be understood by them. Such a work would have to deal with problems of general national concern and reveal the author's favourable approach to the interests of the people in depicting reality.[18]

The most important concept of Soviet art, at its present stage of development, is the principle of *partiinost'*. Iu. Barabash asserts that 'communist *partiinost'* is regarded as the highest form of *narodnost'* of literature.'[19] According to one of the leading Soviet ideologists, M. Suslov, 'Marxist-Leninist *partiinost'* is a principle which implies a consistent implementation of a scholarly, objectively truthful analysis of social phenomena. At the same time it guides scholars and helps them to take up the most correct social-class positions and to combine scholarship with the interests of the revolutionary struggle of the working class and of all workers, and with the aims of building communism.'[20]

It is evident that the political and ideological nature of the principle of *partiinost'* is explicit and that Marxist-Leninist philosophy is supposed to form the foundation of any artistic creative activity in the Soviet Union. In line with the above B. Suchkov is able to assert that '*partiinost'* is the most consistent expression of an author's world-outlook; one that should determine his position in the social struggle, and the system of social ideals for the sake of which this struggle is carried on.[21] Academician M. Khrapchenko elaborates the concept more explicitly by saying that 'the most important characteristic of the principle of *partiinost'* is expressed in its open defence of socialism by the author; the defence of the cause of the working class and the people which is implemented under the leadership of the communist party.'[22]

Although the terms *partiinost'* and *narodnost'* have always been prominent in official Soviet literary terminology, the use of these notions has been re-emphasized in post-Stalin Russia, with the term *partiinost'* being used in the current literary discussions with new and increasing vigour. The use of the concept of *partiinost'* is not limited to internal aesthetic needs only. It has also become the guiding principle in the ideological struggle with the West and with those representatives of socialist and communist parties who do not necessarily agree with the policies of the Soviet state in general and, in particular, with Soviet theories of art.

Leading theorists of Soviet literature take great pains to demonstrate that political and economic coexistence and cooperation do not lead to a rapprochement in the realm of ideology. B. Suchkov, M. Khrapchenko, and others come out strongly against the so-called 'de-ideologization' of art. Suchkov rejects the theories of convergence between Western and Soviet literatures and cultures. He claims that the objective of such theories is to 'subordinate the spiritual development of socialist states to bourgeois ideology; to destroy the boundaries and ideals of the socialist consciousness.'[23] Representatives of Western communist parties, who disagree with certain aspects of Soviet literary theory and practice, are similarly attacked. The French literary theoretician, Roger Garaudy, and the Austrian communist, Ernst Fischer, are singled out for particular attention in this respect. The Chinese are not forgotten in the discussion on the essence of socialist culture and literature. They are accused of attempting to prove that Soviet literature has abandoned the principles of socialist realism and turned to the position of bourgeois humanism.[24] The Soviets claim in turn that socialist realism has been replaced in China by a 'combination of revolutionary realism and revolutionary romanticism.'[25]

Communism is no longer viewed, even in the Soviet Union, as a homogeneous movement with one centre in Moscow, and the interests of different national communist parties are no longer synonymous. The principle of *partiinost'*, as presently applied in the Soviet Union, is intended to serve the objectives of the Soviet brand of socialism and the policies of the Soviet state only. It may be possible, therefore, to replace the general and vague term of communist *partiinost'* with the more specific designation of Soviet *partiinost'*.

There is a distinction between the application of the principle of truthfulness to life in use several decades ago and present practice. In the forties it presupposed the compulsory portrayal of reality in its 'revolutionary development' which resulted in an embellished picture of life. It implied the depiction of reality as it should be rather than as it is. Today many Soviet writers give a truthful picture of reality and they emphasize the negative aspects of Soviet life. This does not mean in the least that Soviet literary scholars accept the truthful depiction of life by an author as a definite expression of realism in art. Referring to the statement of Engels, who declared that 'realism assumes not only truthfulness of details but *accuracy of rendition* of typical characters in typical circumstances,' G.N. Pospelov postulates that the essence of realism 'must be seen not only in the "validity" of the content of the work, but in its "historical concreteness."'[26]

Thus, truthfulness and validity in general are not regarded as synonymous with socialist realism, because it is suggested that 'truthfulness does not necessarily make a work of art realistic.'[27] It is assumed, therefore, that only the realism which accurately renders typical characters in typical circumstances could be regarded as truthful. Thus much of Soviet literature, particularly the literature which depicts the everyday life of Soviet man and emphasizes the negative aspects of Soviet society, is viewed as not complying with the requirements of socialist realism because the situations presented there are supposedly not typical of Soviet life and therefore are not truthful in a theoretical general sense. A. Dubrovin asserts that 'a typical artistic image is synthetic, but it does not copy blindly the values existing in life ... The art of socialist realism accentuates and bases the selection of material on the principle of *partiinost'* ... *Partiinost'* determines the aesthetic mechanism of typification.'[28]

Such an approach to the problem of the typical in art is based on statements of nineteenth-century classical Marxist philosophy as well as on Lenin's theory of reflection, which minimizes the importance of the irrational component of human perception. According to Lenin, the road to objective truth 'goes from live perception to abstract thinking, *and from there to practice,*'[29] and only the perception which appears in its unity of sensation and reflection could be regarded as valuable. In other words, typical truthful reality is not what the author's intuition perceives, but rather the product of the writer's rational analysis of his intuitive and irrational emotions; an analysis which is supposed to be executed in conformity with the requirements of Marxist-Leninist philosophy as well as with the ideological and political objectives of the Communist Party and the Soviet state.

The discussion of the theoretical foundations of Soviet literature is at least a partial reflection of the general changes in the values and in the life of Soviet society which are taking place in post-Stalin Russia. It is also an expression of the disparity between the theoretical premises on which Soviet society is allegedly founded and the practical realities of daily life. The evolution of Soviet literature in the 1970s could thus be characterized by two peculiar traits. On one hand there is the disparity between literary theory and practice. On the other hand, theory has ceased to guide the writer in his selection of the subject or of the artistic means whereby he is to implement his artistic designs.

The development of Soviet literature is a process in which socialist realism evolved from being a realistic method of presentation, in which the reflection of reality was 'typical,' to an ideological and emotional affirmation of certain phenomena and the expression of a certain world-view. The definition of socialist realism as a theoretical notion is now so broad and vague that it is even difficult to regard it as an aesthetic category. Indeed, according to Iu. Barabash, 'socialist realism is the one and only method of Soviet literature (of contemporary literature, at least). But this method has many facets. One of its facets is romanticism.'[30] A. Ovcharenko, in contrast, views 'romanticism as an independent artistic method within the broad framework of socialist art.'[31]

At the early stages of the development of Soviet literary theory, socialist realism was often set against revolutionary romanticism. 'There was a long and heated discussion on the relation between Socialist Realism and revolutionary romanticism, the outcome of which was that the latter was recognized as an essential ingredient of Socialist Realism. This view was advocated by Gorky, in whose work elements of revolutionary romanticism had always been prominent.'[32] Now if one is to view romanticism, as A. Ovcharenko suggests, as an independent artistic method distinct from socialist realism, one admits that there is a difference between the notion of socialist realism and that of socialist and Soviet art in general. One also admits that indisputable guidelines, to separate works of socialist realism from other Soviet works of art, are required.

The inability of literary theory to provide the direction and stimulus necessary for the development of Soviet literature is offset, to a degree, by the continuous effort of the Soviet administration (i.e. the bureaucracy in charge of the creative arts) to provide ideological leadership and to promote indoctrination. Scholars, writers, and party organizations meet frequently to emphasize the ideological importance of literature, and to discuss the means by which the role of literature as an educational medium can be enhanced. Similarly, Soviet periodicals and the daily press devote much space to the treatment of problems of literature and art, and make a concentrated effort to discuss Soviet literature in the context of the ideological and political requirements of Soviet life.

The resolutions of supervisory organizations usually stress the relevance of socialist realism to the development of Soviet literature, but without specifying what this term actually means. This is a situation which no longer mystifies anyone who is in touch with Soviet literature. Writers continue to write, hoping that their works will overcome the hurdles of editorial control and will bypass the vigilant eye of the censor; meanwhile, most critics and literary scholars probably see little distinction between the criteria of socialist realism and the prerequisites of *partiinost'* in art. *Partiinost'* is in essence the feature which sets Soviet literature apart from both Russian pre-revolutionary and Western literatures, and which draws a line sharply dividing socialist realism from any other artistic method.

On a recent visit to the Soviet Union I had an opportunity to interview over a dozen prominent Soviet writers and literary scholars with the purpose of clarifying the essence of the theoretical notion of socialist realism. To my amazement and dismay I received no two identical replies. Creative writers displayed a general disregard for literary theory, while literary scholars expressed a number of divergent opinions, echoing the views aired in the general literary discussion which is taking place in the Soviet periodical press. Most scholars agreed, however, that in order to comply with the requirements of socialist realism it is imperative that a positive social background be present in a work of art; that the depiction of personal and social ills be presented in a manner in which there would be no doubt that these shortcomings are not necessarily typical of Soviet life; and that there is in the background a force which is able to help rectify all social imperfections and to solve most personal problems.

In the heyday of the Stalin era the literature of socialist realism was aimed towards the future, tending to infuse the reader with a positive faith in a glorious future after the universal victory of communism, as well as with a confidence in the correctness of the historical path chosen by the Soviet people. Today socialist realism is a literature of affirmation. It is supposed to affirm the Soviet way of life and to justify the policies of the Communist Party and the Soviet government. Therefore one of the few requirements for Soviet art accepted by all Soviet theoreticians is that a work of literature not be anti-Soviet and that it should not question the political and ideological foundations of the established order of things.

Max Hayward suggests, in his article on 'The Decline of Socialist Realism,' that 'it is evident that the development of Soviet literature over the last 18 years has led to the slow dissolution of Soviet literary theory.[33] I think that it would be more accurate to say that the evolution of Soviet literary theory in the last decades has led to both an increasing emphasis on the principle of *partiinost*' (with a simultaneous dilution in the requirements of socialist realism), and to an ever-growing disparity between the theory and practice of Soviet literature (each of them developing its own way, without much regard for each other). In this respect, at least, the Soviet literary scene has come closer to that in the West, where literary theory endeavours to explain literature rather than to serve as an obligatory guide as to how literature is to be written. There remains however, this major difference between the West and the Soviet Union: in the former, literary theory and practice are free from political and ideological interference; in the latter, they are not.

It is evident that while the importance of literary theory in general and of socialist realism in particular is stressed continuously in the Soviet Union, literature is mainly judged today not by its compliance with Soviet theoretical notions, but rather by its adherence to the present-day ideological and political objectives of Soviet art. The forthcoming discussion of literary texts illustrates this supposition convincingly. Soviet writers deal in their works with a multitude of subjects and apply a variety of artistic techniques. But as long as these works are written by pro-Soviet writers, and as long as they do not reject explicitly the Soviet way of life, such works appear in print regardless of the level of their artistic quality. It is unnecessary to say that in the heyday of socialist realism literature was also judged by its adherence to the immediate ideological and political objectives of the Soviet state. But it is necessary to add that in those days the special mechanism for enforcing literary policy was much more powerful than the one now in operation, and no disparity between dogmatic theoretical notions and literary practice was then possible.

LITERARY PRACTICE

The bulk of the Russian prose appearing in official Soviet publications deals with three major time spans in the development of the Soviet state: the historical and revolutionary past, the Second World War, and today's reality. Much of the literature dealing with the revolutionary past and with the Second World War is written in the spirit of socialist realism and *partiinost'* in art. Many works extol the war effort and dedication of the Soviet citizens. They emphasize the pride of the people in their army, and promote the ideological and political values advocated by the Communist Party. It is necessary to point out, however, that a number of writers depicting the historical past approach these events from new and unconventional positions and interpret them in a manner contrary to that accepted until recently in Soviet literary scholarship.

Characteristic in this respect is the creative work of one of the leading Soviet writers, Sergei Zalygin. Zalygin treats the revolutionary movement in Siberia in an innovative manner, often giving precedence to the personal element of human nature over the significance of social and political upheavals (see the discussion of his work in chapter 4). Frequently at the centre of his work are controversial characters who are in conflict with society and who seek counsel within themselves. The theme of the nonconformist individual is a recurring subject in the literature in which the Soviet past is described. The controversial protagonists of such works are usually placed in circumstances in which they are doomed to failure, but the authors do not condemn them; they sympathize with them and respect their integrity and honesty. As an example of such a protagonist one could single out the teacher Gediminas, the main hero of the 1976 Lenin Award–winning novel *Poteriannyi krov* (The Lost Shelter) (1972) by the Lithuanian writer Jonas Avyžius.[34]

The action in *Poteriannyi krov* takes place during the Second World War. The novel is set in the Lithuanian countryside, where the conditions and moods are reminiscent of those experienced by the Russian people in the period of civil war. Avyžius renders well the life at that time in the Lithuanian village. He shows that most Lithuanian peasants were against the Russians, and that many supported the Germans, and even, deep in their hearts, expected the Americans to come and to save them. He shows that there were still decent people ready to risk their lives in order to help and to save others, but that most cared only for their own well-being and survival.

At the centre of the novel is the teacher Gediminas. The essence of the novel is expressed in his tragedy. He wants to remain uncommitted and to preserve his national identity; he wants to be honest with himself and with others. He tries to act in a rational manner, but it appears that he is drawn into the course of events despite himself and against his own wishes. It appears that the little man is trampled upon by the powerful forces of history which do not take into account the personal desires of the individual. Gediminas wants to have clean hands, and yet he is forced to kill in self-defence.

The tragedy of Gediminas is central to the whole novel because in his tragedy is embodied the tragedy of all Lithuanians, and perhaps of all small nations. The desire of a small nation situated between two major powers, to preserve its independence and its own particular identity, is often doomed by the very nature of the struggles taking place. In the conclusion of the novel Gediminas is forced to join the partisans whom he had previously rejected. He joins them not out of conviction but rather due to the circumstances which do not tolerate the existence of a third force. The message of the ending is unmistakable: you have to join those who are powerful, and who are, by the virtue of their force, considered to be just and right, otherwise you are doomed for destruction. It is evident from the novel that the author sympathizes with his hero. He almost identifies with him, and only in the very end makes him reluctantly join the Soviet side.

Poteriannyi krov is a realistic novel, but it is not written in the conventional style of realistic prose. The story is related by several different narrators. The author frequently shifts from first-person to third-person narration. The depiction of events is often impressionistic. The style of the novel is not conducive to detailed characterization but its structure and the unorthodox evolution of its plot render well the spirit of the times in which much is spontaneous and left to chance. The novel definitely appears to be unconventional, even modernistic.

Poteriannyi krov is certainly a mature work of art, in which the personal tragedy of the main hero blends perfectly with the tragedy of the Lithuanian people. The subject matter is relevant to the Lithuanian national experience; yet there are parallels with Soviet prose in which the past of the Soviet state is approached from new positions and reassessed.

The Second World War continues to attract the attention of many Soviet writers, and works of prominent authors as well as war memoirs by generals and soldiers alike continue to fill the pages of Soviet literary journals.[35] The 1970s have witnessed the appearance of the memoirs of Marshals V. Chuikov, A. Vasilevskii, V. Shatalov, and A. Novikov. A number of prominent prose writers have turned out works depicting the war effort of the Red Army and the Soviet people. Konstantin Simonov's trilogy *Zhivye i mertvye* (The Living and the Dead) (1959, 1964, 1971); Aleksandr Chakovskii's *Blokada* (Blockade) (1969–1975); works by Iurii Bondarev and Vasil' Bykov (discussed in detail in chapter 3), and Anatolii Anan'ev are all based on the experience of Soviet soldiers and officers in the last war.

It is possible to notice, however, a certain evolution during the last decade in the pattern of depicting these events. Many writers began to introduce controversial protagonists and to complicate their plots, while others began to question the effectiveness of the Soviet army and its leadership in the early stages of war. The depiction of the difficult life of the simple soldier and of his human reaction to danger and to death has become an important component of war literature.[36] In addition, a number of writers traditionally associated with war literature began to trace the fate of their heroes in the post-war period, while others turned to the portrayal of Soviet reality today. The only important writer who remains true to his subject, by dealing almost exclusively with different facets of war experience, is the Belorussian Vasil' Bykov.

The most controversial literature appearing in the sixties and seventies is that depicting Soviet reality. This literature could be regarded as 'socialist in content' because it describes the life of Soviet society which, according to the Soviet constitution, has entered onto the path of socialism. This literature, however, has generated much official criticism because the bulk of it does not conform to the requirements of *partiinost'* in art. In general terms, Soviet writers dealing today with post-war Russia can be divided into two broad groups: one group depicts the life of the Soviet countryside, while the other group describes different aspects of city life.

The literature produced by the writers associated with the so-called 'village prose' stands out most prominently. The works of Fedor Abramov, Vasilii Belov, Viktor Astaf'ev, and Vasilii Shukshin, published in the 1960s and early 1970s, are well known in the Soviet Union as well as in the West.[37] Most of these works describe the difficult life of the post-war Russian village and the character of the Russian peasant who has preserved his inner purity and high moral qualities despite all difficulties. Some are written in the spirit of nostalgia for the good old life of the past, and for the values associated with it. These works often juxtapose the countryside with the city, with the latter being viewed as an intruder which disturbs the natural life of the village and the normal course of development. It is evident that 'village prose' questions the very foundations of Soviet society and the main course of its development, which is identified with urbanization and technological progress.

It is publicly acknowledged in the Soviet Union that the pages describing the life of the peasants in the remote Russian village belong to the best literature created after the Second World War. In recognition of the above, Fedor Abramov was presented in 1975 with the State Award for Literature for his trilogy *Priasliny* (The Priaslins) (1958–73).[38] And yet, if one is to view the award in the context of current literary activity, it should be regarded as a reward for past merits rather than an encouragement for the future.

It should be seen in this light because of the shattering attack which has been directed by official Soviet circles at 'village prose' which appeared on the scene at a time when the ethical and idealogical values of Soviet life nurtured in the period of the 'personality cult' of Stalin were in disarray. The post-Stalin period was characterized by a re-evaluation of old Soviet values and by the appearance of interpretations of historical and social phenomena which, while contrary to those officially acceptable to the party, were tolerated by its leadership. Among these trends of thought was a renewed interest in certain values advocated by the adherents of the nineteenth-century Russian *pochvennichestvo* (native-soil movement) and Slavophilism. This was coupled with a militant defence of the patriarchal character of the peasantry as opposed to city culture.[39] Another extreme interpretation saw the intelligentsia as the 'leading class' of society, destined to lead the people to social progress.

The discussion and arguments among the neo-Slavophiles, the proponents of intellectualism, and the adherents of the official version of Marxism-Leninism in the arts reached their greatest intensity in the early seventies, and apparently it was decided to stop this before it went too far. In November 1972, Dr A. Iakovlev came out with a sixteen-column article in *Literaturnaia gazeta* (Literary Gazette) in which he strongly denounced all those who deviated from the class approach in the interpretation of literature and artistic values. He claimed that the advocates of the 'roots' approach visualized the countryside in the form of the Russian village of the distant past. According to Iakovlev, 'the exaggerated admiration for the past leads to a situation in which the class contradictions in the history of a nation are overlooked; it conceals the contradictions and the irreconcilability of progressive and reactionary tendencies; it dulls the vigilance in the contemporary ideological struggle.'[40] Iakovlev came out against the use of terms such as 'national spirit,' 'national feelings,' or the 'people's national character' when they bore no relation to the class character of past events. He asserted that writers who used such phraseology and adhered to the values of the patriarchal past represented vestiges of an obsolete consciousness that was closely related to petty bourgeois nationalism.

Soviet literary criticism has attacked 'village prose' along similar lines. While most critics agree that 'village prose' is one of the most serious trends in current Soviet literature, they also claim that it is not serious enough for today's reality, i.e., that it does not encompass the most important problems.[41] Critics agree that it is dangerous and even unethical to forget the nation's past, but they argue that 'one cannot live in the past alone, and, therefore, since "village prose" is devoted to the past, its one-sidedness and limitations are perceived with increasing intensity.'[42]

The main criticism of the 'village prose' is conducted along sociological lines. It is claimed that the Soviet countryside has changed so much in the last decades that the situations and characters depicted are not representative or typical of reality now. It is suggested that it would be more logical for literature about the Soviet village to show the changes for the better taking place there, rather than pointing out and emphasizing the shortcomings of the past. In a highly regarded article which analysed 'village prose,' E. Starikova asserted that 'the juxtaposition of the themes, problems, and images of "village prose" with the findings of sociologists about the situation in the countryside leads one to the impression that there is a striking contrast and contradiction between them.'[43]

Ivan Afrikanovich, the main hero of V. Belov's *povest'* (novelette) 'Privychnoe delo' (That's How It Is) (1966)[44] has been singled out for particular criticism. Belov's protagonist is a likeable and harmless fellow. He is a war veteran devoted to his hard-working wife Katerina, the mother of nine children. Ivan Afrikanovich earns little, however, and he likes to take a drink. Belov does not idealize his hero; Ivan Afrikanovich is a man with human weaknesses and shortcomings who is apparently content with his fate because he lacks the determination necessary to change the course of his life. Belov, however, is attacked because 'he does not show the path which would help Ivan Afrikanovich to become a real master of the land. Moreover, intentionally or unintentionally, Ivan Afrikanovich's inability and lack of desire to change anything in his "accustomed way of life" is poeticized in the story. The idea of *partiinost'*, the idea of an active intrusion in life, of a reconstruction of life on socialist foundations, does not find any adequate expression in 'the people' as portrayed by V. Belov.'[45]

One can appreciate the concern of the Soviet literary establishment with the future of 'village prose.' Indeed, for the first time in decades literature of high artistic quality has been created by Soviet writers; but instead of agitating the reader to join in the struggle for the revolutionary transformation of society, it takes him back into the past. Instead of imbuing him with the spirit of dedication to communism, it evokes a nostalgia for past values. The essence of 'village prose' is expressed in the fact that it approaches and interprets life not from the positions of class and communist morality, but rather upholds the view that there are ethical values which transcend national and class boundaries.

Despite criticism of the sociological aspect of 'village prose,' the countryside continues to attract the attention of many Soviet writers. In a speech delivered at the Fourth Congress of Russian Writers, which took place in Moscow during December 1975, the editor of *Oktiabr'* (October), Anatolii Anan'ev, decried the fact that most works submitted by young writers for publication in his journal dealt with the Russian village of the past; that the writers extolled in their works the good life of the past and the virtues of their grandfathers.[46] To counteract this situation some writers have begun to describe the new Soviet village in a manner which emphasizes the socialist transformation of the countryside and the corresponding rise in the level of both agricultural production and peasant living standards.

Such an idealized picture of the Soviet village is encountered in Anan'ev's novel *Gody bez voiny* (Years without War) (1975).[47] Its main protagonist, a retired colonel named Korostylev, goes to a remote village in the Penza region to visit his brother-in-law, Pavel. Pavel, in the past the chairman of a *kolkhoz*, has been demoted to the position of a simple tractor driver, and yet he is happy with life. He is respected by his wife and children; he lives in abundance and has a car. He sleeps well and enjoys his work. Korostylev envies him. He himself has run away from Moscow so as to escape the frustrations of city life and the family problems which have beset him there. Anan'ev's novel, however, is artistically inferior to the literature characteristic of the main stream of 'village prose.' Anan'ev tells us a lot in his novel but he depicts little. He raises a number of important social and personal problems which are developed inadequately, and he introduces a multitude of characters who do little and are therefore soon forgotten.

The early 1970s have witnessed a certain disintegration of 'village prose' as a literary trend. A number of writers, in the past closely associated with 'village prose,' continue to write about the Russian countryside; but their works lack the unifying ethical message which was characteristic of this literature in the heyday of 'village prose.' Thus, for example, Evgenii Nosov describes in 'Usviatskie shlemonostsy' (The Helmet Bearers from Usviaty) (1977)[48] life in a remote village in central Russia in the first days of war in 1941. The peaceful life of the peasants is suddenly disturbed by the realization that war affects everyone. First the young people and later those who are older are called up to join in the struggle against the enemy.

The slowly flowing narrative, rich in poetic and folklore elements, reveals the story of the main hero, the simple peasant Kas'ian. Kas'ian joins the army and by doing so becomes united with his fellow countrymen in their common struggle against the enemy. Kas'ian's fate is now closely bound with the destiny of his nation. Nothing heroic happens in the story; the conscripts are not even shown reaching the front line. But the tender scenes of parting and the symbolically portrayed foreboding of a dangerous and unpredictable future remind the reader of the horrors of war which can intrude upon the peaceful life of a nation without advance notice. Nosov's story is an example of how the combination of the village theme with the patriotic war theme produces a story which can exert an emotional and didactic effect on the Soviet reader.

Another writer whose creative activity has been in the past closely related to the village theme in literature is Sergei Krutilin. Krutilin is best known for his novel *Lipiagi* (Lipiagi) (1967)[49] in which the narrator, a village teacher, renders in the form of a chronicle, covering some thirty years, a sensitive and subtle picture of his native village and its inhabitants. In the seventies, Krutilin's main attention has been devoted to the city and, in particular, to the war theme. He has finished his trilogy *Apraskin bor* (The Apraskin Forest), based on his personal experiences in the Second World War. The first part of the trilogy was published in 1968 under the title *Leitenant Artiukhov* (Lieutenant Artiukhov),[50] while parts two and three, *Kresty* (Kresty) and *Okruzhenie* (The Encirclement), were published in 1975 and 1976 respectively.[51]

Krutilin's trilogy is in the main stream of Soviet war literature. Each part has a different conflict, and takes place at a different time and location, but the ideological message of the novel is expressed by the character of the commissar Chuev, who appears in all parts of the trilogy. The commissar's determination and his dedication to the people represent the leading role of the Communist Party in the nation's struggle against the German invader. Krutilin claims that with the conclusion of the trilogy he takes leave of the war and returns to the subject of the Russian countryside,[52] but it remains to be seen whether his promised new novel will reach the artistic level of his village narrative of the sixties.

In the meantime Krutilin published another story about the life of an unsuccessful Moscow painter. Igor' Kudinov, the main protagonist of 'Masterskaia v glukhom pereulke' (A Studio in the By-Street) (1978),[53] is a fifty-year old artist who has created in his whole life only one masterpiece: a portrait of a woman he really loved. But Kudinov's love was short lived and so was his artistic inspiration. Subsequently he spends most of his time in filling commercial orders, work which is very profitable and which requires artistic technique, but no talent or inspiration. It is possible to conclude from Krutilin's latest story that artistic inspiration, love, and hard work go hand in hand while creating to order (*na zakaz*) kills love, requires no inspiration, and does not encourage hard work! Instead, high profits from work requiring little talent foster a life-style full of corruption and ethical shallowness.

One Soviet writer whose name is closely associated with the village theme is Viktor Astaf'ev. Astaf'ev's loosely connected autobiographical narrative 'Poslednii poklon' (The Last Respects),[54] which the author has been writing for over twenty years, is set mainly in the pre-war and immediate post-war Siberian countryside. It is a tribute to the writer's grandmother, Katerina Petrovna, who is a selfless, compassionate, and dedicated woman who represents the best spiritual and human qualities of the Russian people.

'Poslednii poklon' was written in the best traditions of 'village prose' of the 1960s, but Astaf'ev's works of the seventies strike also a new cord. His war story 'Pastukh i pastushka' (The Shepherd and the Shepherdess) (1971)[55] is complex and controversial. Its main protagonist, Lieutenant Kostiaev, dies not from wounds received in battle but from his inability to cope with internal spiritual discord and the cruel realities of war. Astaf'ev's interest is directed in this story not at the portrayal of soldiers' heroism and military exploits but at the tribulations of the human soul and at the devastating effect war has on its participants. No wonder 'Pastukh i pastushka' has satisfied few Soviet critics. Many accuse the writer of pessimism and pacifism, and attack him for selecting for the main hero a character who is not typical of the Soviet officer fighting against Nazi Germany.

Astaf'ev's most recent work 'Tsar'-ryba' (The King of the Fish) (1976)[56] is set in Soviet Siberia. It is a narrative composed of a number of stories of different length unified by the theme of man's relationship to nature. Astaf'ev contrasts in 'Tsar'-ryba' the callous and utilitarian approach of the city-dweller to nature with the attitude of the natural man, the Siberian hunter and fisherman, who senses intuitively his harmony and unity with nature and who views himself as a part of the omnipotent natural world.

'Tsar'-ryba' questions the usefulness and the effect of the rapid intrusion of technological progress in the remote regions of Siberia. It calls for the protection of nature and for the preservation of natural resources. It makes one realize that the rapid transformation of Siberia is not only an ecological problem but an ethical one as well. With the physical transformation of the distant Siberian regions the native people become unprooted and lose touch with the land and the values which nourished their bodies and spirit for generations. Astaf'ev's prose, in which the author's language blends with the local dialect of the Siberian peasant, is highly individualistic. His slow-flowing narratives and meditative digressions prompt the reader to think about the relationship of good and evil, about the inconstancy of fate, as well as about the path of each individual in life.

Another example of a writer who entered literature through 'village prose' but who has presently diversified his range of themes is Vladimir Tendriakov. A number of Tendriakov's recent plots are set in small towns, and the leading characters are young people. In some cases Tendriakov juxtaposes two generations: young, uncorrupted teenagers, and their fathers, who have abandoned spiritual values for the more tangible advantages of this world. In 'Vesennie perevertyshi' (Spring Turn-Overs) (1973),[57] the thirteen-year old Diushka Tiagunov represents the gentle and selfless approach to nature and to human life. With his childish mind he tries to inquire into the very essence of man's existence; his concerns are generated by a genuine interest in the future of man. Under the influence of his son, Diushka's father, an engineer and an important man in town, learns to appreciate the complexity of human nature and the fact that there are differences between men. He realizes that there is something good in everyone, and that everyone has the right to remain himself.

'Tri Meshka sornoi pshenitsy' (Three Bags of Weedy Wheat) (1973)[58] is a story set in 1944 in a remote district in northern Russia. The young wounded demobilized soldier Zhen'ka Tulupov wages battle for justice and common sense against the local bureaucrats who are overridden by corruption and complacency. The local leaders are insensitive to the suffering of the peasants, justifying their callousness by their dedication to a higher cause. In reality they are concerned only with their own well-being without regard to the fate of the people.

In 'Noch' posle vypuska' (The Night after Graduation) (1974),[59] the action takes place exactly thirty-one years after Germany's initial attack on the Soviet Union. The plot is set in motion by a valedictory speech delivered at the matriculation celebration at a local school by the best student, Iulechka Studentseva. In her speech she challenges the school; she says that although many different doors are open to her for a brilliant future, the school taught her everything except what was the most important, the ability to make a choice.

The action in the plot develops simultaneously among two different groups of people: the teachers and the pupils. The teachers, shocked by Iulechka's pronouncement, argue about the merits and shortcomings of their teaching methods, while the students, left to themselves, take a bottle of wine and go to the city park to celebrate the important event. They gather near a monument to the fallen soldiers but they hardly notice it. Instead, their celebration turns from an intimate gathering into a bitter quarrel. We are shocked to learn that under the cover of external friendship so much jealousy and antagonism, secretiveness and envy could be hidden – even among close school friends who grew up together. 'Noch' posle vypuska' reminds us that although there is a chasm dividing the old from the young, there is also an abyss separating one human being from another one. We are all different. Young people today usually have high aspirations and good intentions but what is good for one is not necessarily good for another.

The theme of youth is also the main subject of Mariia Prilezhaeva's story 'Osen'' (Autumn) (1977).[60] And again the young are in the fore of the struggle for justice and moral purity, while their teachers and parents are ready to compromise their consciences to further their station in life and position in society. The principal of a local school intimidates one of his better teachers and forces her into early retirement in order to make room for the protégé of a local bureaucrat. Although, under the pressure of the young, the evil-doers are eventually unmasked and truth appears to be victorious, the cause is not eradicated and there is no guarantee that people will not in future continue to act in their old ways.

Tendriakov's most recent work, 'Zatmenie' (Eclipse) (1977),[61] is dedicated to the study of the city intelligentsia. It is, in the main, about the life of a new class of people, well educated and with a solid professional background, people with deep roots in post-Stalin Russia. The depiction of their milieu reflects the changes taking place in the Soviet Union in the last decades, but it also indicates that technological progress makes life easier, perhaps, but not necessarily happier than before.

'Zatmenie' is a story about love, but within the context of an unsuccessful marriage we are exposed to a number of monumental problems which have concerned Tendriakov for many years, but to which he has as yet no solutions. The main protagonist of the story, Pavel Krokhalev, is a twenty-nine year old scientist. He spent all his youth dreaming about a big love, but when he finally encounters Maiia, the woman destined for him, he realizes that happiness is elusive. A person can fall in love at first sight, but it can take many years before two people can establish a mutual understanding, the lack of which can destroy even the most beautiful feelings of love. Pavel's wife deserts him soon for a religious seeker and preacher, a man who talks a lot but does very little. She yearns for a spontaneous love which comes from the heart, while Pavel is a man whose love is rational and inspired by the mind of a scientist. Maiia loves the unexpected and hates the premeditated, while Pavel prefers logic and order. As a scholar he searches for the truth and could not live in an illusion.

Pavel's unhappiness leads him to search for an explanation of his problems. He realizes his own insignificance in relation to nature and eternity but he questions his role in life. Man needs something to believe in, something to live for, even if it is an illusion, a lie. The hard logic of daily life and the realization that there is nothing to live for because in the end there is only death make life unbearable. In conclusion Pavel asks the eternal question 'whether one man can understand, respect, and love his fellow man?' and he replies that 'perhaps there are such people, but in real life it is difficult to meet them – they are illusory.[62]

The problems of man's essential loneliness, of his complex nature, and of his relationship to his environment permeate most of Tendriakov's recent works. Many of his heroes seek an outlet for their frustrations and energies in religion while others seek happiness in love. Most of them fail to satisfy their aspirations. The plot of 'Zatmenie' covers six months between two lunar eclipses in 1974. The evolution of the love affair between the two main protagonists symbolizes a progression from one darkness, which was supposed to become transformed into a light of happiness, into another darkness in which there is little hope for the future. There is little optimism in the epilogue. There is darkness in the physical environment, coupled with an eclipse in the personal fortunes of the main hero.

As an example of a novel in which the life of Moscow intelligentsia in post-Stalin Russia is depicted, one could single out Aleksandr Kron's *Bessonitsa* (Insomnia) (1977).[63] The main protagonist of the novel, the forty-nine year old doctor of sciences Oleg Antonovich Iudin, who was in the past a general of the army medical services, now occupies an important position in a scientific research institute. The action in the novel takes place after the Twentieth Party Congress and it deals with problems generated by Stalin's abuse of power. Alongside of this, Iudin's personal life story is told. The novel is narrated in the first person by the main protagonist, and we do learn a great deal about him and his relations to others; yet his deliberations and meditations appear to be subjective and biased, and his judgment of others is always a reflection of his own interests. He projects himself in a positive light, criticizing those who do not live up to his expectations; but fails to take note of the woman who loved him truly, and to realize that he is the father of her daughter.

Bessonitsa is an interesting novel with a number of personal and social conflicts. Artistically, however, it is not too impressive. There are a number of sub-plots, depicting in detail various secondary characters. They are interesting in themselves but slow the flow of the narrative and distract the reader's attention from the main conflict. Instead of increasing dramatic tension, these digressions decrease the intensity of narration and destroy the artistic unity of the plot. Moreover, the author's obsession with superfluous detail distracts his attention from the major problems in the novel, leaving the reader without a clear conception of the motives which guide the main characters in their actions.

Bessonitsa is in step with the trend in Soviet literature towards the comparison of the Soviet Union and the West in terms that are no longer general or abstract. Authors now endeavour to project a realistic picture of certain aspects of life in the West. They try often to combine the positive with the negative in order to create a semblance of objectivity, but conclude their comparison with a statement confirming the superiority of the Soviet system. Iudin, the son of exiled Russian revolutionaries, is well suited for the purpose of depicting the West. His mother was buried in Paris, and he himself was born there. He still feels an emotional attachment to that city, and his impressions of it, and of the West in general, certainly have a degree of objectivity. Iudin's impartiality is an illusion, but his alleged sentiments in relation to his native city enhance the reader's faith in the truthfulness of the projected picture of the West.

Both 'Zatmenie' by Tendriakov and *Bessonitsa* by Kron are narrated in the first person, the narrators speaking mostly about themselves. But while 'Zatmenie' is conceived primarily as a problem study, *Bessonitsa* is rather a character study. In both works the authors cover too much ground in too little space. Tendriakov exposes us in his story to monumental problems to which it would be futile to seek solutions within the narrow confines of a *povest'*. Kron, on the other hand, introduces us to a number of different characters, with some of whom we become intimately acquainted, but he fails to delineate clearly the main course of the conflict. In 'Zatmenie' there is a certain artistic balance in the plot, while in *Bessonitsa* the lack of artistic proportion in the author's conception of the plot is evident.

Still another picture of the Soviet intelligentsia is presented in the novel *Druz'ia* (Friends) (1975)[64] by Grigorii Baklanov, a writer until recently almost completely concerned with the war theme. The action in the novel takes place in the mid-sixties in a regional centre in Russia. The main protagonists are two close friends, Andrei and Viktor, who work together on an architectural project for a new subdivision in town. Andrei appears to be an honest man, dedicated to his family, to his job, and to his friends. He places truth and personal integrity above all else. Viktor is a hypocrite and office-seeker, ready to sacrifice truth, self-esteem, and his best friend Andrei for the sake of advancement on the job.

The picture of the bureaucracy in this provincial town is well drawn. It appears that each locality has its own 'personality cult,' the majority worshipping those who are in power at any given moment. It is not important what one represents, but rather the position he is in; and the moment a person is out of favour everyone is ready to forget him. The title of the novel is ironic; we are introduced in the beginning to two close friends, but as the action progresses little remains from their former friendship, with one acting behind the back of the other in order to further his own egotistic interests. Artistically, after the main conflict is introduced, the relationship between the 'friends' is removed from the surface and the depiction of the main protagonists is replaced by a number of sub-plots and secondary characters.

The picture of the Soviet intelligentsia in *Druz'ia* is little different from that depicted in many other works. We learn from these works that there are many young people, born and educated after the revolution, who lack ethical principles and who are ready to sacrifice anything and anyone in order to get on, to be promoted at any price, and climb the ladder of social and professional advancement which also guarantees material well-being. We learn from such works about careerists who permeate Soviet society and who influence and shape the lives of others in a manner useful and satisfying to themselves but detrimental to public interests and to the society of which they are a part.

Another theme which has attracted many prominent writers, including a number who until recently have been identified with 'village prose,' is that of everyday family life in the Soviet city, or the so-called *byt*. Works such as 'Predvaritel'nye itogi' (Preliminary Results) (1970)[65] and 'Dolgoe proshchanie' (The Long Goodbye) (1971)[66] by Iurii Trifonov, 'Pustoshel'' (Weeds) (1973)[67] by Sergei Krutilin, *Iuzhno-amerikanskii variant* (1973)[68] by Sergie Zalygin, 'Sladkaia zhenshchina' (The Sweet Woman) (1973)[69] by Irina Velembovskaia, 'Dozhd' v chuzhom gorode' (Rain in a Strange Town) (1973)[70] by Daniil Granin dwell on the negative aspects of daily life. Faithlessness, infidelity, divorce, broken homes, abandoned children, and permissiveness are the rule rather than the exception in these works. Most of the characters are unethical and concerned only with their own well-being. As the title 'Pustoshel'' indicates, this literature deals with the 'weeds' of society. What is amazing, however, is that among the weeds are encountered people from all walks of life; simple workers and leading scholars, writers and painters as well as party dignitaries.[71]

The main heroine of Velembovskaia's 'Sladkaia zhenshchina,' Anna Dob-rokhotova, is a simple worker in a candy factory. The 'sweet' in the title refers to the sweet smell of her body as well as to the fact that she attracts men. We are told that Anna had a number of love affairs, bore a son, and even managed to get a husband, but she could not hold on to him. She is a shallow woman and her physical qualities could not make up for her lack of spirituality.

'Pustoshel',' by the already mentioned Sergei Krutilin, is different from anything previously written by this author. The main heroine of the story is Marina, the wife of the painter Gleb Makoveev. Gleb deserts his wife and daughter and marries the art critic Larisa. Marina in turn carries on a casual affair with a young student until Oleg, a friend of Gleb, arrives from the *tselina* (virgin land) and proposes to marry her. Marina and Oleg live together for a while, spending lavishly the money he earned at the *tselina*. They announce their forthcoming marriage but it turns out in the end that Oleg has no money left, no job, and no permission to stay in Moscow. Oleg goes then to the north, leaving behind a frustrated Marina. There are no positive characters in 'Pustoshel'.' Most of the families shown are unhappy, and Gleb's friends, the painters, appear to be corrupt, unethical individuals. The actions of Oleg, who could be regarded as a representative of the pioneers of the Soviet *tselina*, are motivated by the desire to earn as much money as possible, and to enjoy life. Krutilin is familiar with the life of the Soviet virgin lands. He is the author of the novel *Podsnezhniki* (Snowdrops) (1961) in which he depicts the life and the struggle of the pioneers in the steppe of Kazakhstan.

The appearance of works such as those discussed above had strong repercussions in Soviet literary criticism. Many claim that the situations presented are untypical and, therefore, distort reality. One critic asserts that 'there is a danger in depicting "only the *byt*" because the *byt* limits the perspective of the artist; it hides much from him, and it smoothens out things for him ... *poshlost'* [a negative or pejorative term meaning roughly 'commonplaceness' or 'Philistinism'] of depiction and characterization prevails in the description of intimate life. Erotic "pranks" are subsituted for the art of psychological analysis. There is no consistent irreconcilable moral judgment of the heroes. Instead there is only superficial censure.'[72] According to some sociological studies, however,[73] the works cited do indeed give a truthful picture of reality, and reflect the failure of the Soviet system to influence beneficially the personal and family life of Soviet man.

Official Soviet literary criticism does not come out against the depiction of everyday life in general; it insists, however, that it should be done in a manner in which there is a fair balance between the positive and the negative aspects of Soviet reality. It is claimed that personal and intimate life should be presented in relation to the heroes' labour and social activity. Works such as 'Zavodskoi raion' (The Factory District) (1973)[74] by Arnol'd Kashtanov and the play 'Stalevary' (The Steel Founders) (1973)[75] by Gennadii Bokarev are often cited as examples in which there is a fair balance between the depiction of home and work, between the social and the personal. 'Zavodskoi raion' is a story of a young family in which the husband deserts his wife and child. The heroine, an engineer, finds in the meantime solace in her work. When the husband returns home, because he cannot find any flat for his new family, the wife receives him with open arms. It is possible to agree that there is in 'Zavodskoi raion' a semblance of a balance of the social and the private but the work is rather weak and its outcome is not convincing.

The main hero of 'Stalevary' is a young apprentice in a steel foundry, Viktor Lagutin. He is hard-working and dedicated to his job. He does not hesitate to expose his foreman publicly for lowering the quality of production in order to fulfil the production quota so that the members of his brigade could receive their bonus. Viktor fights single-handedly against drunkenness and lack of discipline among the workers, for high moral standards in life and work.

It appears, however, that while Viktor endeavours to teach others how to live he is unable to arrange even his own personal life. His marriage is on the rocks. He is deserted and ridiculed by his friends. He is looked upon as a traitor who abandoned the cause of his fellow workers. In the end Viktor is defeated, but we do not get any answer to the ethical question posed by the play.

It appears that the unity and comradeship of the workers, based on material incentives even at the cost of lowering the quality of production and cheating the state, win out over the honest approach of the main protagonist. We have here a clear case of double morality: you cannot harm your friend who works and puts up with all the difficulties of daily life with you; but you can cheat the invisible and impersonal state machine which will probably, in your own understanding, suffer little from your transgression. The danger of such an approach to life and to work is obvious. When it becomes a way of life in a collective state, the state and its economy are torn apart from within; everyone wants to receive from society more than is due to him and to contribute as little as possible.

The depiction of the so-called *byt* in the Soviet Union is not limited to the portrayal of family and personal problems. The young writer Andrei Skalon, in his story 'Zhivye den'gi' (Ready Cash) (1972),[76] gives an artistically impressive account of the urge of an ordinary Soviet man to earn as much money as possible, in a manner which runs counter to Soviet law. The main hero of 'Zhivye den'gi,' Arkania Alfer'ev, is an excellent worker. He has a good job, an apartment, a wife and a son: all the ingredients necessary to make him a happy man. And yet he leaves his job and goes to the *taiga* in search for *zhivye den'gi* – extra money. He exhibits an insatiable thirst for money, and for game, which he sells privately because official Soviet agencies pay considerably less for fur than one can get on the black market.

One of the main themes of 'Zhivye den'gi' is the relationship of man to nature; the grandeur of nature in the *taiga* is contrasted with the insignificance of man and his Philistine objectives. The natural conditions of the *taiga* bring Arkania close to his only companions, the dogs. The struggle for survival makes them mutually dependent on each other, but the irrational dog is a more dedicated and reliable partner than the rational man. The dogs would not abandon their master in danger, while the boss contemplates eating his pets in order to survive. Arkania is guided only by materialistic considerations and he thinks about his dogs in terms of money: how much are they worth? Skalon portrays convincingly the psychology of a hunter: he is a gambler, he likes the element of risk. His preoccupation with hunting is prompted by the desire to get money, but there is also a passion for game and a certain emotional involvement in this pursuit.

The social aspects of the story illustrate convincingly different sides of everyday Soviet life. The Soviet critic Nina Podzorova suggests that Arkania 'is a social type taken from real life. He is a man who exploits his professional training, his ability and skill for his personal use and convenience only. He is a shady dealer who abuses the human aspects of our social law which guarantee every citizen a right to work.'[77] Of course Arkania abuses the law, but then so does everyone in the story by supplementing official earnings with some kind of endeavour which contradicts the law. Arkania hunts and sells most of his prey to speculators, who in turn re-sell the fur on the black market at a further profit. The pilot of a helicopter, who is a well-paid employee of the state, risks his position by taking the hunter into the *taiga* in order to make a few roubles on the side. It appears that breaking the law in order to make extra money has become a part of everyday life in the Soviet Union, a reality to which most Soviet people have become accustomed. Indeed, the Soviet critic V. Litvinov asserts that 'material well-being determines one's consciousness, but it turns out that even at a well-served table could sit spiritually poor people.[78]

Most works of literature depicting everyday reality concentrate on the negative aspects of Soviet life and emphasize the ethical shallowness of Soviet city-dwellers. Soviet theorists of literature are quite concerned with such a course of events, because instead of educating the people in the necessary spirit, such works could produce an opposite result. Too many people could endeavour to justify their own negative actions by following the bad examples set by the heroes of such works. Too many could emulate actions and behaviour which substitute the lack of moral principles and an easy hedonistic life for true ethical values, perseverance, and integrity.

In line with the above it is now claimed in the Soviet Union that the main objective of Soviet literature is to create a new positive hero, a representative of the working people of the period of scientific and technological revolution; a hero who would be realistic enough to be acceptable to the Soviet reader. Such works belong to the much discussed 'labour theme' in contemporary Soviet literature which unfortunately attracts few gifted Soviet writers. It is no wonder, therefore, that many recent works about workers are artistically inadequate. In the words of the Soviet critic Vadim Bocharov, 'there are many interesting books about the contemporary working class ... These works consist of all the required "components" which remain, however, not synthesized; the separate parts do not form any organic whole,'[79] failing thus to satisfy the requirements of good art.

Such, for example, is the novel *Tekhnika bezopasnosti* (Safety Precautions) (1977),[80] by Iurii Skop. It contains enough conflicts for a dozen books, but most are poorly developed. The action in the novel centres around the work of a fertilizer plant in the north of Russia. The main heroes are workers, engineers, and production managers. 'According to Iurii Skop, the notion "*tekhnika bezopasnosti*" [production safety] refers to an odd combination of personal and production relationships in which the motives of personal self-protection prevail: do not touch me and I will not touch you; do not notice when I act badly, and I will overlook your faults.'[81] *Tekhnika bezopasnosti* is supposed to be a novel in which the main subject is the relationship of people in the process of production. 'The author of the novel assures us continuously that work and problems of production are most important to the heroes. He assures us verbally because these problems do not become a part of the heroes' lives; they do not move them.[82]

Having probably realized that production problems are largely prosaic and could not attract the reader's attention for too long, Iurii Skop decided to make up for this shortcoming by including long passages dealing with the protagonists' private lives. This attempted combination of the personal and the social is not successful, however, because instead of relating the heroes' emotional experiences the author describes their behaviour and actions, which are little related to the main theme of the plot. This structural deficiency leads in turn to a lack of stylistic unity and a recourse to the journalistic style of narration characteristic of the so-called *khudozhestvennaia publitsistika* (loosely translated, 'artistic journalism').

Anatolii Krivonosov's *povest'* 'Gori, gori iasno' (Burn, Burn Brightly) (1974),[83] is also about workers. It is artistically superior to *Tekhnika bezopasnosti*; it has all the ingredients required for an interesting plot but it lacks dramatic tension. The main hero, Parfen Loktionov, is an excellent worker and a good family man. He works as a locksmith in a match factory and is promoted to the position of foreman. The new job places him above his fellow workers and secures him a modern apartment in the nearby settlement. Surprisingly, his wife and mother-in-law are against moving from their old house, and against Parfen's promotion. The conflict leads to a break in the family and to the death of Parfen's premature son. 'Gori, gori iasno' shows clearly that technological progress and job advancement do not necessarily lead to personal happiness, and that social status and group or even class consciousness are very important in Soviet society and that there is little in common between the simple worker and supervisory personnel.

The main conflict in the story is between Parfen's personal aspirations and the conservative ideas and habits of his family. It is a conflict in which the desire to serve a social cause leads to personal misfortune and unhappiness. It is perhaps also a conflict to which there is no definite solution because we are not told in the conclusion whether Parfen's resignation from his new job has been accepted and whether his family life returned to normal after the tragedy. It appears that there is little optimism in the ending. Parfen, who is essentially a good man, cannot reconcile the conflict of the social and the personal in his life, and is finally defeated.

Another writer who concerns himself mainly with production problems is Mikhail Kolesnikov. One of his recent novels, *Altunin prinimaet reshenie* (Altunin Makes a Decision) (1976),[84] centres around the disagreement between the young, who strive for change, and the older generation, who are afraid of daring innovations in the operation of a machine-building plant. The plot is complicated by the fact that the main conflict in the novel is between two relatives: the young engineer, Altunin, and his father-in-law Samarin, with Altunin's wife Kira siding with her father.

The novel received favourable mention in Soviet literary criticism. And no wonder: *Altunin prinimaet reshenie* incorporates most of the ingredients required for a work of socialist realism. It has a selfless positive hero who is ready to sacrifice his personal life for a social cause. It also has a happy ending in which the main conflict is resolved to the benefit of society. In addition, most problems are solved with the help of the party organization which leads the people wisely onto the road of progress. There is in Kolesnikov's novel an element of intrigue and the Soviet reader can readily identify with the problems discussed.

But the actions of the protagonists lack psychological motivation and the balance between the personal and social elements in the life of the hero is completely distorted. In addition, the subject of the novel is very topical and it relates only to Soviet production experience. It lacks the universality and concern with general human problems which are the hallmark of great literature, a shortcoming characteristic of much 'production theme' fiction. Viktor Astaf'ev once noted aptly, in his critical remarks on 'Stalevary,' that in such works 'human feelings, suffering, happiness, and grief are replaced by a production battle ... which reminds one not of peaceful life but rather of something similar to what I have witnessed at the front.[85]

The works discussed above, as well as other works on the 'labour theme,' indicate clearly that without treatment of the heroes' personal lives there is very little such works can offer to the sophisticated reader today. Most works about labour and workers are prosaic and uninspiring; their conflicts are often artificial and most readers remain unmoved by them. The Soviet worker lacks the revolutionary fervour, zeal, and dedication more common among the workers of the twenties and thirties. There is, after all, no immediate cause or enemy to unite people in a struggle, no immediate danger to their existence. Accordingly the objectives and the actions of many people, as depicted today, are often petty and vain, guided by the egotistic desire to live better and to enjoy life at any price. This is not to say that all the characters depicted in Soviet literature are negative. There are also positive heroes, but the number of truly believable positive heroes is limited. It is easier to criticize than to praise; it is easier to reject than to affirm. Today's conditions lead to a 'deheroization' of the image of the Soviet worker.

In conclusion it is possible to suggest that whereas one of the main concerns of Soviet literature is the creation of a new positive hero, a new image of man in the period of alleged transition from socialism to communism, most Soviet writers today are preoccupied with the problem of the ethical foundations of Soviet man and society. Most of the works discussed in this introductory survey fall short of the requirements for good art; and the responsibility for moving forward the artistic evolution of Soviet literature falls upon the shoulders of the few talented artists such as Chingiz Aitmatov, Valentin Rasputin, Iurii Trifonov, Vasil' Bykov, and several others.

These writers transcend in most cases the narrow thematic and national confines of Soviet literature by creating works of artistic merit. It is necessary to note, however, that they work in the genre of the story or *povest'*, while the evolution of the Soviet novel lags far behind. With the exception, perhaps, of Iurii Bondarev's *Bereg* (1975) and Sergei Zalygin's *Komissiia* (Commission) (1975) very few novels written and published in the seventies have been considered worthy of favourable mention in Soviet literary criticism. The novel is a literary genre which often requires a broad treatment and interpretation of personal and/or social issues. According to one Soviet critic, however, 'contemporary Russian prose lacks the necessary wide-reaching artistic and philosophic view of reality ... The writer and the thinker in a [current] work of art are usually detached from each other. [This] situation prevents the attainment of major artistic objectives and hinders the process of passing on unchangeable and important spiritual values to future generations.'[86] It is possible to deduce from what we have seen that today's Soviet novel lacks the basic qualities characteristic of great literature: it is very topical; its relevance is limited to a certain period of time only; most important, it lacks subtlety and depth.

2 ❧ Chingiz Aitmatov: Myth and reality

Few non-Russian prose writers in the Soviet Union transcend their national literatures and attain prominence on the Soviet-wide literary scene. A number of those
who do succeed write in their native tongues as well as in Russian, and often
translate their own works from one language into the other. Among such authors in
the Soviet non-Slavic minorities, the Kirghiz writer Chingiz Aitmatov stands out
most prominently. Aitmatov is popular not only in the Soviet Union; he has also
gained considerable prominence on the international literary scene. According to
figures supplied by UNESCO, his works are among those most widely translated into
foreign languages.[1]

Aitmatov was born on 12 December 1928 in the settlement of Sheker, in the
Talass Valley of the Kirghiz republic. During the war, after completing grade six,
young Aitmatov was forced to abandon school and to work on different jobs in his
native village. After the war Aitmatov continued his education. He first attended a
secondary specialized veterinary school and later studied at the Kirghiz Agricultural Institute. After graduation he worked for three years on a cattle-breeding farm
in the Kirghiz countryside.[2]

Aitmatov began to write while still at school. His first published stories, 'Ashim'
and 'Sypaichi,' appeared in 1954, followed by 'Belyi dozhd'' (White Rain) (1955),
'Soperniki' (Rivals) (1955), 'Trudnaia pereprava' (The Difficult Crossing) (1956),
'Litsom k litsu' (Face to Face) (1957), and others. In 1958 Aitmatov graduated from
an advanced course of study at the Gorky Literary Institute in Moscow and became
a professional writer. Aitmatov's graduation coincided with the appearance of his
first collection of stories in the Russian language. This was followed by the publication, in the August 1958 issue of *Novyi mir*, of his famous love story 'Dzhamilia,'[3]
which started, in a way, a new stage in Aitmatov's artistic development.

The appearance of 'Dzhamilia' placed Aitmatov among the most gifted young
Soviet writers, and the reading public began to follow his work with great interest.

In the late 1950s and early 1960s Aitmatov worked as a special correspondent for *Pravda*, continuing at the same time to write prose. A collection of his stories entitled *Povesti gor i stepei* (Tales of the Mountains and Steppes), which included 'Topolek moi v krasnoi kosynke' (To Have and to Lose) (1961), 'Pervyi uchitel'' (The First Teacher) (1962), 'Verbliuzhii glaz' (A Camel's Eye) (1961), as well as 'Dzhamilia,' was awarded the 1963 Lenin Prize for literature. The period of maturity in Aitmatov's art begins with the publication of his masterpiece 'Proshchai, Gul'sary!' (Farewell, Gul'sary!) (1966),[4] for which he won the 1968 State Prize for literature; this was followed by 'Belyi parokhod (Posle skazki)' (The White Steamship) (1970),[5] 'Rannie zhuravli' (Early Cranes) (1975),[6] and 'Pegii pes, begushchii kraem moria' (Spotted Dog by the Sea's Edge) (1977).[7]

In addition to writing prose, Aitmatov is very active in the world of cinematography, being one of the pioneers of the young Kirghiz cinema. He is the head of the Union of Kirghiz Film-Makers as well as the author of the screen versions of many of his stories. He also made an attempt to enter the world of theatre and drama when he wrote, together with Kaltai Mukhamedzhanov, the play 'Voskhozhdenie na Fudziiamu' (The Ascent of Mount Fuji).[8] This was first staged in 1973 by the 'Sovremennik' theatre, in Moscow; and later, in the summer of 1975, in the United States by the Washington Arena Stage Theatre. Aitmatov's position in Soviet literature is firmly established. He is a member of the editorial boards of *Novyi mir* and *Literaturnaia gazeta*, among others, as well as the spokesman for Soviet writers and film-makers in the international cultural arena. And yet, if one is to single out the artistic pursuit most responsible for the development of Aitmatov's creative individuality, one inevitably turns to his prose.

The evolution of Aitmatov's creative mastery is a continuous process which could be characterized as a constant search for new means of artistic re-creation, for new artistic images, and for new narrative techniques. At the centre of his art Aitmatov places man and his relationship to his fellow man, to society, and to nature. Aitmatov does not presume to solve in his works any of the burning problems facing man and society today. He claims that 'by doing the job assigned to journalism and trying to solve economic problems, literature is wasting its energies.'[9] His work, however, is an expression of his personal, social, ethical, and artistic concerns which reflect very much the official Soviet view of social phenomena.

Aitmatov's art has evolved gradually, but there is a common denominator which is characteristic of all his works, beginning with his earliest stories. At the heart of Aitmatov's prose there are always acute dramatic collisions and deep personal conflicts. The author's poetic perception of reality, and an ever-growing intensity of narration are present in all his works. It is sometimes possible to notice in his early stories an oversimplified plot development or a lack of psychological motivation for the actions of the heroes, shortcomings of which Aitmatov managed to rid himself in his mature works. Thus, for example, in 'Litsom k litsu,'[10] the Kirghiz peasant woman, Seide, betrays her husband, the deserter Ismail. It appears that Seide places the importance of the social cause above the value of her personal relationship with the father of her children. It is a solution which finds sympathy with most Soviet patriots, but it is psychologically unconvincing. In contrast, Valentin Rasputin's 'Zhivi i pomni' (1974)[11] pictures convincingly the internal struggle, taking place in Nastena, the wife of a deserter, who rather than betray her husband perishes along with her unborn child.

At the centre of most of Aitmatov's early stories, up to 'Proshchai, Gul'sary!' there are always women. In 'Dzhamilia,' the work which marks the beginning of the steep ascent of the writer's popularity, it is a woman who betrays her unloved husband for a new and real love. In 'Topolek moi v krasnoi kosynke,'[12] the tender and loving Asel' is a young woman who runs away from her native village in order to escape the oppressive patriarchal traditions of her family, but finds little happiness in the more civilized environment elsewhere. In 'Pervyi uchitel',[13] the academician Altynai spends most of her life in the pursuit of her only love, the illiterate teacher Diuishen, a selfless man who helped and saved others but who remained forgotten by all. In 'Materinskoe pole' (Mother Earth) (1963),[14] the main character is the old woman Tolgonai who shares with mother earth the reminiscences of her terrible past. 'Verbliuzhii glaz'[15] portrays the loving and pregnant Kalipa who is deserted by the greedy and wicked Abakir.

There is much in common between the fate of the women protagonists in Aitmatov's early prose. Most of them break with tradition and with the established pattern of life of the Kirghiz village woman. Their actions express the eternal striving for personal freedom and the desire for happiness. These women take their fates into their own hands, but most fail to achieve the desired contentment and tranquillity. There is an element of personal tragedy in the fate of these women. They reach out for a bright future with hope, but many end up in disappointment and despair.

Most of Aitmatov's early stories are narrated in the first person. 'Dzhamilia' is told by the fifteen-year-old Seit, the brother of Dzhamilia's husband. He is a painter, an artist at heart, who appreciates the value of Dzhamilia's love for a total stranger. 'Pervyi uchitel' ' is also a monologue by a young painter who is entrusted by the academician Altynai with the task of making public her life story. 'Verbliuzhii glaz' is told by the seventeen-year-old Kemel'. He tells us about the unhappy relationship between Kalipa and Abakir, who is an excellent worker but an evil man. Aitmatov shows clearly in this story that dedication to one's duties on the job is not necessarily an indicator of fine human qualities in a man. Characters such as Abakir, or Dzhantai from 'Topolek moi v krasnoi kosynke,' foreshadow the appearance of people such as Orozkul in 'Belyi parokhod.' 'Materinskoe pole' is a monologue of an old peasant woman, while 'Topolek moi v krasnoi kosynke' is a tale constructed of three monologues. The two men in the life of Asel' tell in the first person their own version of their life stories, the third narrator being a journalist who listens to their tales.

Young people play a dominant role in Aitmatov's early works. According to the writer, childhood and youth are a time when people are able to perceive best the beauty of our world, and Aitmatov endeavours to present, through the eyes of his young narrators, what might seem to be an uncorrupted and objective view of reality. The mature Aitmatov demonstrates a predilection for narration in the third person. He claims that writing in the first person is an easy way out. It limits the possibilities of an all-round objective evaluation of the heroes, and of the re-creation of an all-embracing picture of reality.[16]

Aitmatov's masterpiece 'Proshchai, Gul'sary!' is narrated in the third person. It is a touching story about the similar fate which befalls two creatures: a man and a horse. Both are defeated by outside forces, vain and greedy to satisfy their own narrow interests. The main hero, Tanabai Bakasov, has all his life sacrificed for the cause of the party, but he is expelled from it for not submitting to the evil pressures of his superiors. The horse Gul'sary is castrated because he would not submit to his new boss who removed him from his natural environment and from his friend Tanabai. In the relationship of Tanabai and Gul'sary is exemplified the bond between man and nature which is, in this case, based not on rational calculations but rather on a warm mutual feeling of attachment and dedication. As in most Aitmatov's other works, there is an element of tragedy in the conclusion of 'Proshchai, Gul'sary!' The old horse dies, while the old man is broken in spirit. Tanabai sits at the dead body of his beloved horse and reminisces about his past. There was little happiness in his life before, and there is not much in store for the future.

There is no question that an injustice has been done to Tanabai; that he has been penalized for the faults of others. It is also evident from the story that he has aged before his time and that he realizes his time has passed. And yet it is not difficult to encounter in Soviet literary criticism interpretations to the contrary. It is often suggested that despite everything, Tanabai remained a dedicated communist and a fighter for the cause of the people. Indeed, it is difficult for Tanabai to wipe out from his memory all his past and to change his views. It is possible to agree with the contention that Tanabai does not reject his ideals. The fact remains, however, that while Tanabai does not reject the party, the party rejects him. We are persuaded by Soviet critics to believe that the misfortunes which befall Tanabai are the result of Stalin's abuse of power, now a thing of the past. We are told that 'the reader knows well about the changes [now] taking place in the life of the nation and the party; about the reestablishment of the Leninist norms in Soviet society.'[17]

According to the story, however, old wrongdoings have not been rectified, and the sources of evil have not been eradicated. The story is placed in perspective by the introductory and concluding remarks of the author. We learn that Tanabai travels to town to see his new grandson. The visit brings him little happiness. His daughter-in-law taunts him for being expelled from the party. She claims that Tanabai's past makes impossible the promotion of her husband. Thus it appears that the ten years which have passed since the Twentieth Party Congress, at which the 'personality cult' of Stalin was denounced, were not enough to re-establish the just treatment of those who, according to their deeds, deserve it most.

Aitmatov's prose of the 1970s, which includes 'Belyi parokhod (Posle skazki),' 'Rannie zhuravli,' and 'Pegii pes, begushchii kraem moria,' can be identified by a number of common traits. Children are at the centre of all these works. In Aitmatov's early stories youngsters are, in a way, outsiders to the main events. They observe reality and tell us about their impressions. In the last three works, children are at the centre of the plots; they are the main heroes. The ethical values professed by adults are measured in relation to their attitude to the young and helpless. Evil and corruption, existing in society, are juxtaposed with the naïve faith in goodness and truth experienced by the young, who have as yet not been affected by the evil influences of their mentors.

All the recent works by Aitmatov are set in a natural environment in which the grandeur of nature is contrasted with the insignificance of man. At the heart of these works are elements of folklore, legends, and Kirghiz mythology. Aitmatov's recent works can be viewed as parables in which minor local events have universal spiritual and ethical significance. In most of them the positive and the good go down to defeat, while evil is victorious. As in his earlier works, tragedy continues to occupy an important place in Aitmatov's art. He regards tragedy as the highest form of artistic expression because it can help us to understand better the distinction between good and evil. Aitmatov asserts that the tragic end of a good hero, which may often be the only noble way out of an existing situation, should by no means be seen as the spiritual defeat of the hero. There is often a high price to be paid for spiritual superiority.[18]

'Belyi parokhod (Posle skazki)'[19] is one of the most beautiful stories ever written by Aitmatov. It is, however, also one of his most controversial works, open to a number of different interpretations. It is narrated on several different levels in which reality and myth are closely intertwined. The main hero of the story is a nameless boy who lives in a mountain outpost, together with his grandfather Momun. The boy has been deserted by his divorced parents and he leads a lonely existence among adults.

His only friend is Momun who instills in him the values of his ancestors by telling him legends of the Kirghiz past. Momun tells the boy a beautiful story about a

Mother-deer who saves two Kirghiz children and leads them from Siberia into the land presently occupied by the Kirghiz people. The Mother-deer saves the Kirghiz tribe from extinction and the Kirghiz people, in turn, worship the deers and protect them from evil. There was in those days a perfect harmony between man and his environment, a natural peace between all living creatures. All this changed when some wealthy people killed a deer in order to decorate their father's grave with its horns. Following the example of the rich, everyone begins hunting down the deer until the few remaining deer desert the land of the Kirghiz.

The boy lives in a dream. He tries to unite the values imparted by Momun's stories with his imagination about the future; the latter being closely related, in the story, to a white steamship sailing on the nearby river. But the boy's dream is shattered. Momun is humiliated by his wicked son-in-law, Orozkul Balazhanov, and he is forced to kill a deer which is sacred to the boy. The boy is shocked; reality for him becomes so unbearable that he decides to become a fish in order to be near his father who is allegedly sailing on the white steamship. Aitmatov juxtaposes in 'Belyi parokhod' the good and the gentle, embodied in the boy and Momun, with the evil forces of society, represented by Orozkul, who is in charge of the outpost. Orozkul is hired to protect nature, but he destroys it. He is a wicked man, greedy for power, a man without heart or moral principles. The plot of 'Belyi parokhod' moves through the subtle interaction of reality and fantasy, the disparity between them leading to the boy's breakdown and to his tragic end.

This is not the first time that Aitmatov has resorted to the use of mythical elements in his narratives. 'Proshchai, Gul'sary!' contained a similar legend. A young hunter destroys all the animals in his native land but he cannot kill the last remaining goat. In pursuit of the animal he is drawn deep into the mountains until he reaches a point of no return. He is enticed and entrapped by the goat who avenges herself on the hunter for killing her mate and her family. The hunter stands above an abyss without being able to move and he begs his father, who comes to his rescue, to kill him and thus save him from terrible suffering. The old hunter kills his son and he sings a lament over his dead body. The story about the hunter and the goat is very poignant and forceful. No one is permitted to tamper with the normal course of nature; no one should try to destroy the beautiful harmony created in our environment. The hunter's lament is essentially an artistic device with the help of which the author renders the tragic, the deep emotional experiences in the life of Tanabai. The lament is sung to Tanabai by his wife upon his return from the funeral of his best friend.

In 'Belyi parokhod,' on the other hand, the myth 'is a conception, a basic layer of the narrative.'[20] It designates the ethos of man's relation to, and his interaction with nature. Myth in 'Belyi parokhod' is central; it is integrated artistically with, present-day reality and moves the main dramatic conflict in the plot. Aitmatov expresses also in this story his own conception of man's relation to his environment. The writer is by no means against technological progress, but he is opposed to the abuse of natural resources. He feels that the penetration of modern civilization into the remote Kirghiz countryside has many drawbacks.

Today, he says, there are in people 'less responsiveness, less compassion, less solidarity ... They forget the good national traditions, and do not value their aboriginal culture.' Aitmatov claims to have met in his life many 'illiterate people who, nevertheless, adhered to principles which are humane in the highest degree. And that is most important.'[21] Aitmatov thus does not equate education with spirituality and he acknowledges that material well-being often leads to ethical shallowness. 'If material things become the only objective of man's existence ... they lead to his degradation. The very essence of man is lost.'[22]

'Belyi parohkod' generated in the Soviet Union a strong and mixed critical reaction. Most critics value highly the beauty of Aitmatov's new story. According to Vladimir Soloukhin, 'Belyi parokhod' reaches the highest level of artistic perfection. He asserts that Momun and the boy are in possession *'of an element of spirituality in life,'*[23] something which is sadly missing in the other characters. But Momun is unable to stand up in defence of his values, and his philosophy of non-resistance to evil suffers complete failure. 'When the poetry, beauty, and dream are destroyed ... the boy could no longer remain there. The beauty does not defeat the people, who are void of any spirituality, but it deserts them – and this, perhaps, may be regarded as its victory.'[24]

Other critics accuse Aitmatov of discussing the important concepts of goodness and evil in abstract terms; some readers suggest even that it would be more logical to have Orozkul placed in jail, provide Momun with a retirement pension, and to have the boy sent to a boarding school. D. Starikov writes in *Literaturnaia gazeta* that the boy's dream and his fantasy are part of his real life, a part without which he cannot live, but according to the story 'reality and beauty, in the form presented here, are incompatible.'[25] And this is mainly, according to Starikov, because 'the essential contradiction between the tale and reality is not *investigated*, as it relates to the boy's fate, but is given rather externally.'[26] Starikov's criticism amounts to a demand that Aitmatov should have shown in the story the practical alternatives available to Soviet man in his approach to spiritual values, and in his interpretation of problems of good and evil in Soviet life.

In an article published several years after the appearance of 'Belyi parokhod,' Feliks Kuznetsov tries to rectify the alleged shortcomings of the critical response provoked by the story, and he endeavours to place the discussion of 'Belyi parokhod' in a social context. He claims that 'at the centre of the conflict in the story is not an abstract conflict of goodness and evil, of Faith and the lack of it, of Beauty and spiritual emptiness, but a very real collision, depicted according to the rules of harsh realism, between Orozkul, who embodies the extreme form of a beastly animal image of a proprietor, and the old Momun ... who is the embodiment of patriarchal ethical principles.'[27] Kuznetsov goes on to say that 'the tragic death of the boy is also a judgment passed on Momun, on his passivity and servility, and his inability to oppose evil.'[28]

Such an interpretation of 'Belyi parokhod' could be regarded as an oversimplification of the meaning of the story, an approach in which the personal traits of individual heroes and problems of general human concern are overlooked at the expense of their social significance. Indeed, it is not difficult to see that Kuznetsov fails to note, in his discussion of 'Belyi parokhod,' that Orozkul is not a proprietor but a Soviet civil servant: a man born and educated after the October revolution, in whom the innate balance of evil and goodness has not been influenced in favour of the latter by his Soviet upbringing.

It is worthwhile to note that the evil in the story is embodied in the actions of representatives of the Soviet state, while goodness is personified in those who adhere to old patriarchal values. The resistance of Momun to evil would also, in a sense, be a resistance to those who represent the Soviet system on the outpost, a fact Orozkul is very well aware of. The old and powerless Momun is helpless in his struggle against Orozkul, whose brute force is supported by the legality of his position.

In reply to his critics Aitmatov wrote: 'I was startled by the fact that the problems posed in the ancient parable about the Mother-deer did not lose their ethical meaning in our own days ... The criterion of humanity is here the relation of man to nature.'[29] Aitmatov continues by saying that the tragic conclusion of 'Belyi parokhod' is inevitable because 'the goodness represented by the boy turns out to be incompatible with the evil of Orozkul. And the boy is only a boy and he could set against the brute force of Orozkul only his passive irreconcilability. The passive goodness of Momun fails, but the boy's opposition to evil remains with him.'[30] Aitmatov asserts that he could not have concluded the story differently. 'Such is the logic of artistic conception which has its own principles and which is outside the author's control.'[31] It is not the only instance where Aitmatov acknowledges the importance of the irrational element in artistic creation. On another occasion he says that 'one can hardly perceive one's heroes with one's pure reason only,'[32] a fact which is highly disputable in Soviet literary theory.

Aitmatov's next story, 'Rannie zhuravli,' is set in a remote Kirghiz village in the difficult days of the Second World War. Most men are in the army and young boys are called upon to do the work of adults. The youngsters work hard and with dedication. They get the horses ready for the spring sowing and move into the steppe, but robbers attack their camp and take away the horses. The boys put up a desperate struggle but to no avail. They are left behind broken, dejected, and defeated.

'Rannie zhuravli' is a story about war and labour, about the relationship of fathers and sons, and about the effect of unpredictable circumstances on the growing generation. The war separates fathers and sons physically, but it brings them closer together spiritually. The young boys idealize their fathers who are away and endeavour to replace them by taking over their responsibilities at home. But 'Rannie zhuravli' is also a story about love and adolescence. According to Aitmatov, 'the main hero, Sultanmurat, goes down to defeat, but the main theme of the story is the birth of a poet in man.' War rages far away, while here two young people discover the meaning of first love.

Aitmatov endeavours to show a young teenager growing and developing into a true poet. The moving force leading him onto this path is his love for the beautiful girl Myrzagul', as well as his love for life in general. The war is destructive and evil forces are victorious but, despite all, the soul of the young man blossoms. The conclusion of the story is tragic but there is a note of optimism in it, a hope that love will overcome all obstacles. According to Aitmatov, 'love in our contemporary world ... undergoes apparently certain changes. It is possible that it has even become too easy, to accessible. I wanted in my new story to draw attention to the fact that this holy feeling should always remain the highest expression of humanity.'[33]

'Rannie zhuravli' is written in the spirit of Aitmatov's earlier works. The intensity of narration grows continuously, reaching its climax on the very last pages of the story. The language is rich in poetic and epic elements and the boys are compared to heroic warriors from the Kirghiz epos. There is a symbolic parallel between spring in nature and the spring in the life of the main protagonists, their first love, and their hopes for a bright future.

The title of the story is significant. The arrival of the 'early cranes' usually heralds a good harvest; it is a sign of good luck. In this case, however, the cranes bring little good fortune. The boys are watched from afar by several outsiders who contemplate something evil. In the night they attack the camp and steal the horses. Sultanmurat pursues them but his horse is killed, while the stolen horses are led away to be sold for meat on the black market. The epilogue of 'Rannie zhuravli' has a parallel in 'Materinskoe pole.' The peasants give away their last grain for seeds for the spring sowing. The deserter Dzhenshekul, who hides in the mountains, attacks the boys in the field and steals the seeds. Tolgonai pursues the thieves but they kill her horse and she remains behind dejected, cursing the attackers.

Aitmatov was too young to serve in the army during the Second World War, and perhaps that is why there is no direct portrayal of military combat in his works. All the same, war is present in an indirect manner in most of his stories. Aitmatov asserts that since antagonistic forces – which may try to resolve their differences by resorting to war – continue to exist in our world, the subject of war remains one of the most vital themes of Soviet literature.[34] Aitmatov juxtaposes in his stories the suffering of simple people and their dedication to the common national cause with the greed and spiritual emptiness of those who want to become rich by feeding on the suffering of others.

Just as in 'Belyi parohkod,' evil is also victorious in 'Rannie zhuravli.' But, according to Aitmatov, he applies in these stories the mathematical method of argumentation in which one proceeds from the reverse position in one's reasoning.[35] It is a method of description which aims mainly at the readers' emotions. The negative characters in such works are victorious and unpunished but the reader is roused by the behaviour and actions of the culprits and he is inspired to fight against them. The indignation of the reader with the negative, in such cases, is much stronger than his sympathy with the positive. Such works stimulate the reader to try to overcome in real life the obstacles encountered by Aitmatov's heroes, a fact which helps retain the educational value of these stories for the Soviet reader.

Aitmatov's latest story, 'Pegii pes, begushchii kraem moria,' is in many respects similar to his earlier works, but it contains also a number of new artistic elements. It is the first mature work by the writer which is not set in his native Kirghiz land, and in which the main heroes are members of another nationality. It is also his first work set in pre-revolutionary Russia, a marked departure from Aitmatov's earlier stories. But this story, perhaps more than any other of his works, transcends local and national confines. It is a work of deep philosophical import to people of any nationality, religion, or age.

There are four heroes in the story, representing three different generations. They are members of a small ethnic group, the *Nivkhi* (Nivkhs), residing on the northern shores of the Okhot sea in the Far East. The basic conflict in the story is simple. The eleven- or twelve-year-old boy Kirisk is taken by his father and grandfather to be baptized in the art of hunting at sea, the main source of livelihood for these people. While on the open sea, far from shore, they are faced with a terrible storm, followed by a dense fog in which all but Kirisk perish.

The story begins with the description of the everlasting struggle between land and sea, two natural forces, each with its own rights. We are told that in the beginning there was in the universe only water, and the land was created from the feathers of the duck Luvr who looked for a place to lay her eggs. Man is usually identified with land, and the struggle between water and earth represents the struggle of man with the dark forces of nature. This struggle is best visible at the seashore where the waves continuously attack the land, only to be repulsed. Young Kirisk is somehow restless at sea. 'He is aware of a danger; he dimly feels his dependence on the sea, and his infinite insignificance and endless defencelessness in the face of this great element.'[36]

Not so his grandfather, Organ. He is tempted by the sea. He knows that a man in a boat is nothing in comparison with the infinite space of the waters, but since man is strong in spirit and he is able to think, he is just as infinite as heaven and earth. Organ realizes that death is inevitable, but he visualizes his death in the form of a return to the Fish-woman who, according to myth, is the mother of the Nivkhs. He constantly dreams about her and he is confident that these dreams will remain with him after his death. He is sure that since the Fish-woman is immortal, the dreams about her are also immortal. Organ sees his immortality in his union with the past, represented by the Fish-woman, and with the future, embodied in his son Emraiin and his grandson Kirisk.

Organ lives what he preaches. He is the first to go to the bottom of the sea in order to make possible the survival of others who are younger. He sacrifices himself physically, but his spirit will continue to exist in the young. He views his death as a reunification with nature, as a return to his ancestors. Organ is a pagan but his convictions are unshakeable. He lives with them and he dies with them. His faith gives him the necessary strength to live honourably and to die without regrets. His vision of the universe and of life in general is based on a simple ethic at the root of which are selflessness, altruism, and a natural honesty with himself and with others.

The fate of Kirisk could be juxtaposed with the fate of the nameless boy in 'Belyi parohkod,' who also lives in the world of nature which is desecrated and abused by the dark forces created by society. The boy in 'Belyi parohkod' perishes because of the ethical shallowness and the wickedness of those who are in charge of his future. Kirisk survives the terrible ordeal because of the spirituality and selflessness of those who are close to him. Momun shares much of Organ's view of life. His reverence for the Mother-deer is strikingly similar to Organ's idealization of the Fish-woman. But Momun cannot withstand the onslaught of evil and he goes down to defeat. Organ's virtue is a passive one, similar to that of Momun, but Momun lives in a time when action is necessary to overcome the evil forces of 'civilization.' The sacrifice of Organ and Emraiin make the survival of Kirisk possible, while the surrender of Momun saves no one.

The message of Aitmatov's latest story is unmistakable. It is primarily an ethical message which is not at all complimentary to our modern society. Technological and social progress have done little to change man for the better. On the contrary, they have prompted him to believe that he is the master of nature and of life, a delusion fraught with dangerous consequences. Organ sought the meaning of life in his identification with nature and in unity with its eternal forces. He regarded himself as a part of nature. For most of Aitmatov's modern heroes nature is only a means to satisfy their material desires and to further their own narrow interests. Organ treats man just as he would treat nature. Man for him is a part of nature. He respects both. Orozkul, also treats man in a manner similar to his treatment of nature. He respects neither; both are to serve him when he requires them, and to be abused at any other time.

In 'Pegii pes, begushchii kraem moria,' just as in 'Belyi parokhod,' reality, legend, and myth are intertwined. The story is narrated on several different levels with a constant transition from the present to the past, from reality to dream. The images selected by the writer strengthen the ethical message of the story, and render well the essence of the main conflict. The tone of the narrative is set in the very first paragraph, in which the eternal struggle between water and earth is defined and portrayed in the form of a front, with one force attacking the other one. The paradox of man's tragedy is rendered in one short sentence: 'It is monstrous, finding themselves in the boundless ocean, they were perishing from thirst.'[37]

The intensity of narration grows in the story continuously. The fog subsides only after all the adults, Kirisk's father, his uncle, and his grandfather commit suicide in order to leave the remaining drinking water for Kirisk. They go down when the boy is asleep. They want to spare him the anguish of witnessing the death of the people he loves. The boy is left alone at the mercy of nature and fate. When he wakes up to notice the shore of the Okhot sea, shaped like a skewbald dog, he is lonely and sad. He realizes that the experience of the last few days and the memory of those who saved his life will always be with him. The author does not describe the return of Kirisk to his native settlement; this would surely be anticlimactic.

Symbolism, myth, and philosophical allegory are artistic devices applied successfully by Aitmatov in his recent works. They raise his stories to a new level of artistry and universality, uncommon until recently in contemporary Soviet prose. Yet his artistic style is not to the liking of many critics and readers. Some accuse the writer of a departure from realism in art and of an attempt to escape from real life, while others come out against the use of different artistic devices with the purpose of concealing a message under their surface.[38]

Aitmatov does not hesitate to rebut such criticism and he comes out 'against the so-called utilitarian everyday "realism" which locks man up in a shell of commonplaceness,'[39] and which limits the writer's artistic scope. Aitmatov decries the fact that many readers fail to appreciate good literature because their tastes 'have been developed and formed by a highly didactic and flatly moralistic prose that canonized and regulated its protagonists and their psychology and behaviour from the standpoint of practical expediency.'[40] There is no doubt that Aitmatov alludes here to the kind of literature which appeared in abundance during the heyday of socialist realism.

A concern with ethical problems permeates Aitmatov's creative path, but nowhere does he deal with these questions with such poignancy as in his play *Voskhozhdenie na Fudziiamu*. The main protagonists of Aitmatov's stories are usually simple peasants or ordinary residents of remote Kirghiz settlements. In

Voskhozhdenie na Fudziiamu the heroes represent the top layer of the Kirghiz intelligentsia. Four old friends meet at a nearby hill, dubbed Mount Fuji, to celebrate a school reunion. It appears from their acrimonious discussion that during the war, when they were all together in the army, one of them denounced their best friend, the poet Sabur, who was subsequently arrested and sentenced to a prison term.

According to Japanese tradition, every Buddhist is supposed, at least once in his lifetime, to climb Mount Fuji to clear his conscience, to have a talk with God, one to one, and admit his sins and transgressions. Similarly in the play, the four friends decide that everyone will open his heart and make a confession. Unfortunately, those responsible for Sabur's fate are not yet ready to admit their faults. It is evident that the man guilty of the denunciation of Sabur is Osipbai Tataev, a doctor of science and the director of an institute. Osipbai declines responsibility for the fate of Sabur. He says that Sabur's predicament is a mistake of history.

Osipbai considers himself a man of his time. Indeed, he is an opportunist – a man of different faces, changing them in conformity with the requirements of the day. He has written a useless dissertation which makes no contribution to scholarship. He keeps up the appearance of a decent family man, in reality living with his wife only because his social position requires him to do so. Osipbai is a leading figure in Soviet society but he is a shallow man without ethical principles. He drifts along the path of least resistance. His actions are motivated purely by the desire to satisfy his material needs. In one of Sabur's poems there is a line: '*Kak cheloveku chelovekom byt'*?'[41] which can loosely be translated as 'How can a man be [become] a [real] human being?'

It appears that, according to the author, people like Osipbai lack the essential qualities which one requires to become a real human being – a sad commentary on Soviet society, which is fertile soil for the breeding of such individuals. It is interesting to note that the station in life and position in society of those present at the reunion are in reverse proportion to their commitment to truth and to basic ethical and spiritual values. Those at the top of the ladder are ever ready to compromise their conscience in order not to disturb the tranquillity of their complacent existence. They are also the first to abandon Mount Fuji in order to escape responsibility when they realize that a stone, thrown by one of them from the hill, has accidentally killed an old woman.

One of the main protagonists in *Voskhozhdenie na Fudziiamu*, the agronomist Dosbergen, retorts in his argument with Osipbai that communism begins at home, that one has first to be honest with oneself and with those who are close to one before embarking upon universal schemes to save humanity. Indeed, Aitmatov constantly emphasizes that only people who have faith in something, who see something beyond themselves or who truly love someone, are capable of discerning the real values from the false ones, and of making the distinction between good and evil. Diuishen and Tanabai sacrifice their lives for communism because their faith in it is unshakeable – they live what they preach. Momun and Organ believe in tradition, in their unity and harmony with nature, and they submit to its forces. Osipbai believes in nothing. He lives in a spiritual vacuum. It is seldom that a person goes to church to pray without actually believing in God; it is repulsive when one preaches to others something one does not believe oneself.

Aitmatov is one of the most popular Soviet writers. He is an accomplished craftsman whose style is laconic and expressive. His prose is realistic but he shuns unnecessary descriptiveness and superfluous detail. His recent stories are artistic re-creations of reality in which the portrayal of real life is integrated with elements of myth, folklore, and fantasy. At the heart of Aitmatov's works are always acute dramatic collisions of great tension, conflicts to which there are no readily available solutions. Perhaps that is why his works are often controversial and the subject of heated discussions.

His position in Soviet literature is special because he represents a new and growing breed of Soviet writers who embody the fusion of ideological uniformity and linguistic and cultural diversity in the Soviet Union. Aitmatov is active in the administration of literature and cinematography both in Moscow and in his native Kirghizia, and is often called upon to voice the official Soviet view on the place of national cultures in the Soviet Union and on their relationship with their Russian counterpart. Earlier, according to Aitmatov, there 'prevailed the vulgar socio-logical rejection of any national values in the cultures of the past ... while now, all of a sudden, a reverse phenomenon is observed. Voices are heard that only national traits are worthy of becoming the subject of artistic portrayal, the description of which is the prime objective of literature and art.'[42]

Aitmatov, of course, disagrees with such pronouncements. He claims that the national traits of any Soviet nationality should also include new aspects of culture, those created by Soviet reality. He is against the prevalence of exoticism, oversim-plification, and the commonplace in the national arts, instilled by pseudo-nationalism rather than by genuine national inspiration. Aitmatov asserts that although the national spirit, present in any artistic endeavour, is very important, one should not be carried away by regarding the national peculiarities of a people as the most important component in the development of art. Aitmatov stresses that 'the evolution of the socialist content is of decisive significance for all our national literatures and arts.'[43] Thus Aitmatov reaffirms the official Soviet proposition which stipulates that Soviet national literatures should be socialist in content and national in form; that they should evolve on the premise of unity of content and diversity of form.

Aitmatov's views on the development of Soviet literature and the arts reflect very much the official Soviet position in the realm of artistic evolution. Nonetheless, a comparison of his theoretical pronouncements with the results of his creative endeavours – which are at least partially produced by the subconscious – give witness to a widespread disparity between the theory and practice of Soviet literature, and to a number of contradictions inherent in the alleged harmony between different national cultures in the Soviet Union.

3 ✤ Bondarev and Bykov: The war theme

The October Revolution was the focal point of most of the literature appearing in the Soviet Union in the 1920s and '30s. Most Soviet writers of that period were born before the revolution, and many wrote about the past from personal experience. The Second World War, 1941–5, has had a similar impact on Soviet literature during the last three decades. There are few Soviet works of literature written today in which the war with Nazi Germany is not discussed, or in which its effect on Soviet man and society is not stressed.

Works of art in which the war is depicted belong to one of the most important trends in Soviet literature, the development of which is encouraged by the literary establishment. Recent Soviet literary criticism endeavours to introduce a uniformity in the critical response to the treatment of the subject of war in literature, but it seems that it is too early yet for a final interpretation and evaluation of this phenomenon.[1] Indeed most works about the war are produced by writers who have been actively engaged in battle and who are, to a degree, influenced by their memories of the war. In addition, works in which the war is described appear in such a multitude of literary genres and styles, and are executed with such a range of artistic skill, that it is very difficult to generalize about them.

Most Soviet critics divide the development of the war prose into three distinct periods. The first is the period of the war itself; the second period includes the post-war era up to the late 1950s, while the third period has not yet reached its end.[2] The literature of the first period is mainly didactic, its principal objective being the mobilization of the people for the struggle with Nazi Germany. The emphasis in most works of that period is on the atrocities committed by the enemy, and the heroism of Soviet soldiers. The authors usually identify with their heroes, prompted by their subjective committment to the cause of their protagonists.

The immediate post-war decade was dominated by Stalinism and there was little possibility of creating literature of any artistic merit. Even those writers and poets who dealt with what might have seemed to be safe themes were often victimized. The difficulties Aleksandr Fadeev encountered with *Molodaia gvardiia* (The Young Guard) or Aleksandr Tvardovskii with his war poems illustrate clearly this situation. In the post-Stalin period, particularly in the 1960s, we can see the development of a new approach to the treatment of the subject of war in Soviet literature. This has been prompted by the appearance on the literary scene of a number of young writers such as Bykov and Bondarev, who began to write about the war only a decade after the actual events. In the meantime these writers matured, refined their art, and developed a new approach to past events. In addition, the death of Stalin and the denunciation of his 'personality cult' made it possible to deal in literature with topics that had until recently been taboo, and to treat them in an innovative and previously forbidden manner.

Thus, for example, the main protagonist of Konstantin Simonov's Trilogy *Zhivye i mertvye* is General Serpilin, a man purged by Stalin in the late 1930s. It is a paradox that only the war with Nazi Germany saves Serpilin from certain annihilation in prison, a fate reserved for most of the colleagues arrested with him, and it is ironic that Serpilin is saved from Stalin's henchmen only to be killed several years later by a German shell. Simonov makes an attempt in his novel to rationalize the defeat of the Soviet Army in 1941 by examining and analysing Stalin's role in the pre-war purges. This is not, of course, the main subject of the novel, but it is something that could never have appeared in print in the USSR before 1953.

Now, with the events of 1941–45 becoming more remote, the literature depicting the Second World War will inevitably be transformed. Writers who draw their artistic inspiration from their personal experiences in the war grow older and disappear altogether from the literary scene. It is possible that in the not too distant future war prose will change completely, and will turn into historical literature. In the historical novel the artistic images reflect the subjective thinking and feeling of the author and his view of history rather than his reminiscences and personal experiences. As it is, the further we move away from the Second World War the more does Soviet fictional treatment of the war reflect present-day reality and a view of the past which is influenced by the changes in Soviet society in the three decades since the war.

This 'filtering' process is perhaps best exemplified in the works of two prominent Soviet prose writers, Vasil' Bykov and Iurii Bondarev. There are many similarities as well as differences between these two writers. Both were born in 1924; both participated in the war in the rank of junior artillery officers; both began to write in the 1950s. In each case it was the appearance of the first war stories that attracted the attention of the critics and of the reading public.[3] Both write only prose: Bykov predominantly stories and novelettes, while Bondarev also writes novels. But that is almost all there is in common between them and the comparison of their literary output could serve as a good example of how similar artistic inspiration could lead two writers to completely different results.

Vasil' Bykov is a Belorussian who writes in his native language as well as in Russian. His works, dealing with the subject of war, stand somewhat to the side of mainstream Soviet War literature, and his style bears marks of his creative individuality. His stories usually cover a short period of time and involve a limited number of characters. His heroes are simple soldiers and junior officers; there is no detailed portrayal of generals or leading commissars in his works. Bykov uses in his stories harsh, precise imagery; his narratives are usually so condensed and terse that nothing could be removed. The writer places his heroes in most unusual circumstances, testing their convictions and ethical values in situations in which there is only one choice, namely, between life and death.

Bykov depicts war in terms faithful to the actual experience of men under fire; he does not resort to the heroic and romantic conventions with which the war theme has traditionally been associated. He rejects the 'naive view, which is common [in Soviet literature], that there is a special breed of people belonging to the "war generation," or that there is an abstract "comradeship between fellow soldiers." '[4] According to Bykov, an army is composed of individuals and war does not mould them into one homogeneous body. He realizes that man in mortal danger is all by himself; that he is a solitary creature removed from the realities of daily life and concerned only with survival. Bykov sympathizes with his heroes but he does not spare them. Many display true heroism inspired by deep motivation, but death is the price to be paid for ethical purity.

Bykov makes use in his works of a number of artistic techniques and methods of narration. There are in his stories flashbacks, internal monologues, minute detail, and psychological analysis. In some stories the action begins with a small group of participants but in the end they all perish and only the narrator survives to tell us his story. Thus in 'Tret'ia raketa' (The Third Flare) (1961),[5] the only survivor, the soldier Lozniak, kills with his last remaining flare another Soviet soldier who by his cowardly behaviour causes the death of his colleagues. Similarly in 'Ataka s khodu' (Full Speed Attack) (1968),[6] the orderly Vasiukov is the only one to remain alive to tell us of his ordeal. Lozniak is a Belorussian, a former member of a partisan unit, who witnesses the Nazi atrocities in his homeland. Bykov is indignant at the injustice of the Nazis; he is enraged about the uselessness of Soviet fortifications in 1941. But he does not question the ineptitude of the Soviet leadership, nor does he probe into the reasons for Soviet defeat.

True to himself, in 'Ataka s khodu,' Bykov is also concerned with the fate of the individual, but here the conflict is placed in a broader perspective. The action takes place in dangerous circumstances and most men are wounded. The commanding officer Anan'ev arranges the exchange of a Soviet soldier, taken prisoner by the

Germans, for a wounded Nazi. The *politruk* Grinevich is furious. Such exchanges are strictly forbidden. He criticizes Anan'ev in front of the soldiers. The argument between the two junior officers is an ethical one. The author contrasts the human qualities of the one with the blind obedience to orders of the other. Anan'ev tells Grinevich that although the man in question is old, and a poor soldier, he is still a Soviet man and a father of four children. Why should he perish? Grinevich remains unconvinced by this argument.[7]

In one of Bykov's most controversial stories, 'Mertvym ne bol'no' (1966) (The Dead Feel No Pain),[8] the narrator Vasilevich is also the only positive hero to survive the terrible ordeal brought about by the ineptness of the Soviet leadership and the stubbornness and cowardice of the security officer, Sakhno. Bykov hates those who urge others to act in an honourable manner but who are themselves shallow creatures without moral principles. Bykov is perhaps ready to forgive the traitor Rybak, the main protagonist in the story 'Sotnikov' (1970).[9] Rybak, in the past a dedicated partisan, risks his own life in order to save his wounded colleague Sotnikov. Rybak is a simple man with little education. He acts impulsively, and even in good faith. He wants to save himself from death by promising to cooperate with the Germans, but deep in his heart he believes that when the time will come he can vindicate himself in the eyes of his colleagues, the partisans.

Sakhno is different. His actions are 'rational'; he blindly follows orders from above. He suspects his fellow officers of treason, and everyone is for him a potential enemy; vigilance and giving orders are a way of life for him. He does not spare the lives of those under his command, but when he is faced with the enemy, instead of shooting himself as he forces others to do, he gives himself up without regrets.

Vasilevich survives the war but he is haunted by the image of Sakhno. On one occasion he encounters a man who resembles the latter closely. Vasilevich follows him but it turns out that this man is not Sakhno in flesh but rather in spirit. The retired officer Gorbatiuk, in the past a chairman of a military tribunal, is one of those who survived the war by fulfilling blindly the orders of Stalin. According to the Soviet critic A. Bocharov, Gorbatiuk is even more dangerous than Sakhno because 'whereas Sakhno is only a man of action, his counterpart tries also to vindicate and to justify the past actions of various sakhnos.'[10]

'Mertvym ne bol'no' is an attack on Stalin and on his followers who maintain that they have done nothing wrong; that the injustices of the past have already been corrected; that they have just obeyed orders and that there was nothing wrong in doing so. It appears from 'Mertvym ne bol'no' that those who serve blindly and with dedication one master will serve as readily another master. Such people have to serve someone, and it is of little importance to them whom they serve at any given moment. At this point it should be noted that not all Soviet critics are as generous in their evaluation of 'Mertvym ne bol'no' as Bocharov is. Indeed, Bykov has been criticized severely for his depiction of the unheroic aspects of the Soviet war effort and, in particular, for his attack on the remnants of Stalinism. The literary bureaucracy dislikes Bykov's clear allusion to the fact that while officially Stalinism has been repudiated, in practice it is still alive.

In other stories, such as for example 'Dozhit' do rassveta' (To Survive till Dawn) (1972),[11] or 'Al'piiskaia ballada' (Alpine Ballad) (1963),[12] there were no survivors at all. All the most important protagonists perish in battle, and this could be one of the reasons for these stories being narrated in the third person. It is interesting to note that in 'Al'piiskaia ballada' the action takes place deep in the enemy's territory, and the main hero, the Belorussian Ivan Tereshka, is a war prisoner who saves a runaway fellow prisoner, an Italian communist girl, by sacrificing his own life. Thus Bykov's innovative approach to the treatment of his heroes is expanded by his selection of protagonists. His main heroes are often prisoners of war and traitors.

Bykov probes for the internal reasons for the actions of those who join the ranks of the enemy, and he illustrates how the fear of death can strip even a brave man of all decency and push him into cowardice and treason. He points out that Sotnikov's fellow partisan Rybak is essentially not an enemy or a scoundrel. His desire to preserve life at any cost is, however, so strong that his fall is inevitable. He is blind to the terrible depravity of his act and this makes it possible for him to help the Germans execute his comrade, Sotnikov.[13] The psychological investigation of the motives for treason is in a way a novelty in Soviet literature. In the heyday of socialist realism, traitors were to be hated and abhorred, and there was little importance attached to the reasons for their actions.

Many works by Bykov, published in the last decade, are devoted to the Partisan theme,[14] a subject close to the hearts of most Belorussians. Bykov treats his heroes and develops his plots in a manner novel to Soviet partisan literature. It is even possible to say that Bykov is able to apply his artistic skill without the constraints of subjectivity because he himself was never a partisan; and yet he describes the difficult life of the guerrillas with such passion and intensity that many readers are sure that he was one of them.

In a number of works, such as for example 'Mertvym ne bol'no,' 'Obelisk' (Obelisk) 1972), or 'Volch'ia staia' (The Wolf Pack) (1974), there is a visible connection between the past and the present, between the war scenes and peaceful life today. We often encounter the same protagonists many years after the war, and we realize that those who suffered and contributed to the war effort most have been least rewarded for their tribulations. It may even appear to the unsuspecting reader that the young generation is indifferent to the suffering of those who made their peaceful life possible. This is evident in particular in 'Obelisk,' a story about children and their teacher who all eventually perish in the war.

The main hero, the teacher Moroz, continues to teach under German occupation and succeeds in instilling in his pupils high moral values and a hatred of the enemy. When an attempt by Moroz's pupils to blow up a bridge fails, the Germans promise to release the youngsters if only their teacher will come forth and surrender. Moroz is at this time in safety, in the forest with the partisans. He is advised against joining his pupils; it is clear that his surrender will save nobody. All the same he feels that his place is with the children, that it would be easier for them to face death all together. He has instilled in his pupils the values for which they are about to perish, and he can not let their faith in their teacher be shaken. After the war a monument is erected to the memory of the children while their inspiration, the teacher, is considered unworthy of such an honour. For many years he has been looked upon as a traitor; one of those who gave himself up to the enemy without a fight. The Soviet authorities have overlooked, of course, the fact that the heroism of Moroz was of a superior nature, that he sacrificed his life for humane reasons.

'Obelisk' was apparently written under the influence of Tolstoy, but the influence of Tolstoy on Bykov is not limited to the theme of children only. Bykov admits that his interest in the subject of man at war and his concern with ethical problems also are due in part to Tolstoy's influence.[15] Bykov deals, however, with ethical problems of a particular kind, namely, the ethics of war. This is particularly evident in a work such as 'Kruglianskii most' (The Krugliany Bridge) (1969). It would appear that the main objective of man at war is to defeat his enemy and to survive. That is perhaps so, but Bykov asks: at what price? It is obvious that he is against those who save their lives by selling their consciences. In 'Kruglianskii most' this problem is posed with poignant intensity. The simple peasant lad and partisan, Stepka, rebels against those who sacrifice the life of an unsuspecting boy in order to get credit for an illusory military exploit.

The dramatic intensity of the situations depicted and the controversial nature of the ethical conflicts presented by Bykov make his prose vulnerable to the kind of criticism which is usually motivated by ideological and political considerations: something which cannot be overlooked by even a writer of Bykov's stature. This is probably one of the reasons for the change which is visible in Bykov's most recent works. It is not difficult to see that his last stories 'Volch'ia staia,' 'Ego batal'on' (His Battalion) (1976)[16] and 'Poiti i ne vernut'sia' (The Road with No Return) (1978), lack the harsh formulation and solutions of ethical conflicts characteristic of Bykov's earlier works. It is possible that age or pressure of official criticism and editorial control have mellowed Bykov's most recent prose. It has begun to lose its distinctive quality, one characteristic of which is a plot in which only one solution is possible for the conflict presented. This change in Bykov's art, often coupled with certain artistic shortcomings, is encountered in his latest stories, which may indicate that Bykov's talent has difficulties in adapting itself to the demands of the times.

'Ego batal'on' is in many ways similar to Bykov's earlier works, and yet it is different and closer to the mainstream of Soviet war literature. The main hero, and the only one with whom we become familiar, is the commander of an infantry battalion, Captain Voloshin. He is the highest ranking military protagonist in all Bykov's works. Unlike most of Bykov's earlier stories, the emphasis in 'Ego batal'on' is on Voloshin's responsibility for his battalion. He has on his conscience the life of the soldiers and he is dedicated to the protection of their well-being. He knows that war requires sacrifices, but he is against futile and unjustified losses. Voloshin refuses a senseless order by the regimental commander Gun'ko to attack a hill fortified by the Germans, and for this audacity is removed from his position. It is paradoxical that Voloshin has to fight on two fronts: against the Germans as well as against his own superiors. The latter are vain and heartless and concerned only with immediate and illusory military success, regardless of the price to be paid.

The dramatic conception of the plot is based on the fact that no matter how hard Voloshin tries to protect his soldiers, the death of people in war is inevitable – a situation which leads to a conflict between Voloshin's responsibility to his superiors and his responsibility to his own conscience; between his sense of duty and his loyalty and dedication to those whose fate has been entrusted to him. Voloshin tries hard to remain true to himself and to his ideals, and to reconcile the contradictions between duty and conscience, but he is not always successful in this endeavour. At the end of the narrative the wounded Voloshin refuses to go to the hospital and remains with the few survivors of his battalion. His only companion is his dog Dzhim who appears to be a better and more reliable friend than most of the people around. Voloshin could have been killed in battle but his fate was to live and he survived. Bykov concludes his story by saying that chance has the power to kill man but not his humanity, the very quality which distinguishes Voloshin from his cowardly and vain assistant, Lieutenant Markin, and brings him closer to his dog Dzhim.

As opposed to most of Bykov's previous plots in which the war conditions are unconventional, 'Ego batal'on' depicts a classic war situation. There is a front line, and the enemies face each other across the field. The author describes in minute detail one day in the life of a battalion, and the problems facing its commander during that day. But this seeming simplicity of plot does not work as well as it should, and on the last few pages the author tries to tell us what he has obviously failed to show through the actions of his artistic images. Thus we are hastily told that Gun'ko is removed from his position of regimental commander and that Voloshin's actions are vindicated by an unnamed general. It is only possible to surmise that Bykov adds these concluding remarks in order to avert impending criticism. And yet even this does not save the situation. One critic identifies Bykov with his protagonist, and accuses him of passing judgment on a war situation about which he knows nothing. How could Voloshin know and judge the motivating factors which guide his superiors in their decisions, when he surely lacked the necessary qualifications and information to do so?[17]

In his most recent story, 'Poiti i ne vernut'sia,' Bykov returns to the partisan theme. The story covers only several days in the war experience of the two central protagonists, the partisans Zosia Noreiko and Anton Golubin. Zosia is on a reconnaissance mission to the rear of the German army, while Golubin, who is allegedly in love with her, follows the girl without the permission of his superiors. He pretends that he wants to help her, but he goes with the hidden intention of deserting the partisans and finding for himself a quiet and secure place in the territories occupied by the Germans. But Zosia refuses to cooperate with Golubin and a life-and-death struggle ensues between them.

The story has many artistic qualities more characteristic of the younger Bykov. Elements of suspense, intrigue, harsh realism, and tension are predominant in the story. As on many earlier occasions the writer contrasts those who are weak in body but strong in spirit with those who are physically strong but ethically shallow. As opposed to his earlier works, however, Bykov fails here to resolve the main conflict in the plot and leaves his readers guessing at the outcome. The author employs a number of melodramatic scenes in which Zosia and Anton attempt to kill each other; but in the end both survive and continue along separate paths. The ending is certainly not in the spirit of the young Bykov, who never hesitated to disclose to the reader the whole truth, without regard to its tragic intensity and harshness.

Bykov's prose brings to the reader a grim message about the terrifying experiences of war and of its effect on those involved in it. We learn from his works that real war heroes are not always understood or appreciated by those who were never faced with decisions in which the only choice was between life and death. We learn about real heroes who save others at the risk of their own lives but who never live to be rewarded for their actions. Bykov implies that real war heroes are not necessarily those who are hailed as victors and march on parades with their chests covered with decorations. Most real heroes are dead.

Iurii Bondarev's war prose, unlike Bykov's stories, is very much in the mainstream of Soviet literature. This is not to say that Bondarev does not react to changing realities. Indeed, he does, but only in keeping with the general evolution of Soviet literature. In addition, Bondarev is a Russian writer and a respected member of the upper echelon of the Soviet literary establishment: his innovations, therefore, bear the stamp of official approval.

The art of Bondarev is distinctly different from that of Bykov. Many of his works are dramatic in conception and, just as Bykov's stories, cover a short time span. There are, however, usually a multitude of protagonists whose characterization is often superficial. Bondarev is also concerned with justice and ethics, but he presents his conflicts in a manner lacking the dramatic intensity characteristic of Bykov's works. In Bondarev's novels the ethical problems in which individuals become involved are often secondary to major political conflicts and military confrontations in which thousands participate.

Bondarev creates in his novels a number of conflicts and poses many problems, but most of them are unresolved and his works often raise more questions than they answer. Bondarev claims that he is 'almost convinced that an artist should not "solve" any problems. Perhaps he should only pose them, point them out'[18] to the reader. It is evident that Bondarev follows here in the steps of Chekhov, who stated on numerous occasions that it is the duty of a writer to present a problem but not necessarily to solve it. Chekhov's reader, however, has the necessary tools to seek his own solutions to the problems posed, while Bondarev's reader is often left in the dark, and in some circumstances no solutions are possible to the conflicts which form the foundation of Bondarev's plots.

The evolution of Bondarev's prose has been in step with the times. It would, perhaps, be more correct to say that it has followed the changing times, rather than inspiring and revolutionizing the development of Soviet literature. Thus Bondarev's well known novel *Tishina* (Silence) (1962)[19] appeared a number of years after the death of Stalin and the denunciation of his 'personality cult,' when the problems it raised were no longer a secret to anyone in the Soviet Union. The novel gives an episodic account of two short periods of time, three and a half years apart. Many characters are soon forgotten because they are inadequately drawn and appear only for the purpose of moving the plot. Bondarev succeeds, however, in creating a special atmosphere characteristic of the times. It is an atmosphere of helplessness, of stagnation, in which silence is the only road to survival.

The main hero of the novel, the demobilized officer Sergei Vokhmintsev, is expelled from the Party and from the institute where he studies, and his father, an old communist, is denounced by a money-grubbing neighbour and is arrested. Sergei fights for justice but he faces a blank wall. Those who could help him sympathize with him, knowing that he is not guilty, but they are intimidated and prefer to keep silent in order not to antagonize those in power. After his expulsion from the Party Sergei contemplates the past and asks himself 'Why? Socialism is a good which emerges from the development of humankind. Communism is the highest good. And the evil? It clings to our feet like a leech. How can people like Uvarov, Sviridov ... belong to the Party? Perhaps because people like Lukovsky and Morozov exist?'[20]

Lukovsky, the director of the institute, and Morozov, the dean, are good honest people but they are afraid of the bully, the Party secretary Sviridov, who terrorizes everyone with his continuous calls for vigilance in the struggle for ideological purity. Bondarev hints that the apathy of the silent majority is instrumental in creating evil and injustice. He does not tell us, however, what other course could be taken in the circumstances. The conclusion of the novel does not inspire one with much hope, and yet one Soviet critic suggests that the novel ends on an optimistic note. We are asked to believe that 'although the novel ends with Sergei's defeat we all understand well that his defeat is temporary, and that the main ethical victory is on his side.'[21] Everyone is of course entitled to his own opinion, but the optimism of this critic, who wrote his article twenty-five years after the initial events, has little in common with the actions in the novel and with the fate of its heroes. The year 1949 was a dark one in Soviet history, with little hope possible.

In Bondarev's next novel *Goriachii sneg* (The Hot Snow) (1969)[22] we witness the author's return to the war theme. He portrays in the novel one day in the life of an artillery detachment on the Stalingrad front. The action shifts between two different groups of people. One group is composed of junior artillery officers and soldiers, the other, of generals and commissars. In the juxtaposition of Lieutenants Kuznetsov and Drozdovskii, Bondarev endeavours to illustrate how personal character traits influence the actions of various people in battle.

The portrayal of the senior officers is intended to give us an insight into the general mechanics of war, and into the motives which inspire generals in their actions. Following the example of Simonov, Bondarev selects for the position of army commander a controversial person, General Bessonov, whose son has been taken prisoner by the Germans. General Bessonov appears to the outsider a stern, dispassionate man, but he is strict with himself and just with others. He carries a heavy burden in his heart. In the eyes of many, including the security officer Osin, the fate of his son places his reliability as a leading commander under suspicion.

Further, in all probability also under the influence of Simonov, who portrays a meeting between General Serpilin and Stalin, Bondarev depicts Stalin meeting Bessonov before the latter's departure to the Stalingrad front. In general terms the character of Stalin appears in a positive light, but some of his comments reveal his despotic nature and his desire for unlimited power. When the question of Bessonov's son comes up in their discussion, Stalin admits that his own son has also been lost without trace; but he adds that such things do happen, people disappear in war – it is only important that they do not become traitors. Before his departure Bessonov is asked by Stalin why he is so skinny. 'Is it because you have your own point of view? ... or perhaps an ulcer?'[23] Stalin alludes obviously to Bessonov's opinions about the purges of the 1930s, which do not coincide with Stalin's own view of the events.

Artistically *Goriachii sneg* is little different from Bondarev's war prose of the late fifties,[24] but there is an innovative approach to the selection of protagonists, as well as an endeavour to place local events in a broader perspective. Bondarev investigates in this novel the complexity of human relations in conditions of war, but he gives less prominence to the depiction of military exploits. The writer attempts also to draw a symbolic line uniting simple soldiers and generals in their dedication to a common cause, emphasizing thus the ideological message of the novel. This message is enhanced by the portrayal of the Commissar Vesin, a man of superior qualities who loses his life in a battle with superior forces.

Bondarev's most recent novel, *Bereg* (1975),[25] is the author's response to the calls for a revival of the Soviet 'synthetic' novel, a novel philosophical in conception and psychological in nature, written in the true spirit of classic Russian and Soviet literature. *Bereg* is also in tune with the spirit of détente in Soviet relationships with the West and with the reality of the existence of two separate German states. It was the most discussed work of literature in the Soviet Union in 1976, and it is certainly new to Soviet literary experience. It is set in a Western country, and the action in its two parts takes place twenty-six years apart. The first part takes place in the concluding days of the war, in May 1945, in the vicinity of Berlin, while the second part takes place in 1971, in Hamburg.

Only two protagonists appear in both parts of the novel: the young artillery officer Nikitin, who becomes in part two a famous Soviet writer, and the German girl Emma Herbert, with whom Nikitin has a casual affair in 1945, and who later becomes a proprietor of several bookstores and a promoter of modern literature. The two parts of the novel are linked by the efforts of Emma, who has treasured the memory of her first love for twenty-six years and who initiates the invitation to Nikitin, whose books are being published in West Germany.

In 1945 Nikitin and his colleague, Lieutenant Kniazhko, saved the lives of Emma and her brother Kurt. Kniazhko refused to kill defenceless German youngsters who could not be blamed for Hitler's crimes just because they wore military uniforms, but was himself killed by the bullet of a vicious Nazi hiding with the young soldiers. His murder was provoked, however, by the cowardly action of a Soviet sergeant.

The war scenes in *Bereg* are reminiscent of Bondarev's earlier novels, but most of the conflicts are unconventional and have been influenced by present-day requirements. Thus Kniazhko is presented as a man of ethical purity ready to risk his own life in order to save his enemies, and even Soviet critics have to acknowledge that he is an idealized hero.[26] Now, over thirty years after the war, when the existence of two German states is an accomplished fact, the depiction of the relationship between the Soviet army, fighting the Nazis, and the simple German people has been modified, and an effort is made here to separate the Nazis and ss troops from ordinary German citizens, who are often shown in a positive light. In 1971 in West Germany, Nikitin and his friend and companion, the Soviet writer Samsonov, are exposed to the 'evils' of Western civilization. They participate in personal and public discussions on the essence of Soviet and Western literatures and civilization, and in the comparison of different values and philosophies of life. Nikitin appears to be moderate in his views. He searches for a meeting point between divergent philosophies. Samsonov, on the other hand, attacks viciously his hosts and argues with Nikitin. Nikitin agrees with his German editor that people are not perfect and that no one knows the 'whole truth,' a proposition which makes Samsonov furious and provokes a violent disagreement and ideological confrontation between the two Soviet writers. The Germans suggest that as soon as Soviet society reaches the level of material well-being achieved in the West, it will be plagued by problems similar to those besetting Western society, a proposition to which the Soviet writers have no satisfactory reply.

Bondarev is an experienced writer and yet the novel has its artistic shortcomings. The integration of the war scenes with those taking place in 1971 is far from perfect. The philosophical discussions between Soviet and German intellectuals are often incoherent and inconclusive, an indication that the writer is not on firm ground when dealing with controversial problems of the day. The novel poses more questions than it answers, but Bondarev is a master of creating atmosphere. While reading the novel one has a feeling that there is an invisible wall dividing East and West. People are on different shores; they apparently strive to come closer together, but characters such as Samsonov make it impossible. On the personal plane there seems to be the possibility of communication; on the social plane, however, the rapprochement is much more difficult.

Nikitin's venture to the West is a failure. He parts with Emma in a touching scene at the airport, but he completely antagonizes Samsonov. Nikitin seems to have reached an impasse. He apparently suffers a heart attack on his way home, a fact not made explicit. Nikitin has suffered from a heart ailment and cannot endure any physical or mental stress. He does not reach Moscow alive; instead, he gets to the other shore where all is peaceful and quiet.

When asked why it is necessary to conclude the novel with the death of the main protagonist, Bondarev gives an evasive reply. He claims that 'an explanation according to which he could not endure the psychological and nervous pressure would not be entirely correct ... but when I imagine a different ending for the hero, everything receives a different colouring, and the title of the novel *Bereg* becomes meaningless.'[27] It is evident that the author cannot take his hero any further. Nikitin is a man of certain ethical principles, a man who seeks answers to controversial questions and searches for an understanding of life by and within himself – a thankless task today. It would be of no use to have Nikitin return to Moscow and have him exposed to public scrutiny and criticism for his ideological vacillations.

But if Nikitin's ideological purity may be questioned, Bondarev does not leave any doubt as to where he stands personally in relation to his hero and to the problems discussed. He claims that the philosophical and ideological discussions between Soviet writers and German editors depicted in the novel are a condensed version of a number of similar encounters he had an opportunity to have himself while visiting the West. He points out that there have actually been no discussions in these meetings, but rather an open attack on the Soviet Union and the Soviet way of life. He claims that there is presently in the West a new wave of anti-Sovietism which is connected with the support of the so-called 'dissidents' in the USSR and of the alleged struggle for human rights in the Soviet Union.[28]

His statements have obviously been induced by political considerations and may throw a new light on the original tone of the novel. It is not difficult to see that the statement may have been provoked by the new developments in Soviet-American relations, and also by the 1976 presidential election in the United States, which resulted in a new approach to problems of human rights and to problems of international policy and détente.

The appearance of *Bereg* generated a heated discussion among Soviet literary critics. Most view the novel as an experimental work; they reject Samsonov's dogmatism but at the same time do not accept Nikitin's view of life as an adequate expression of Soviet ideology. One critic suggests that *Bereg* is perhaps 'one of the best Soviet novels, "the most important book" to appear in recent years,'[29] but he also asserts that it is a very complex work which combines in itself a number of elements characteristic of different literary genres and styles. Another critic claims that while there is an inherent connection between Bondarev's last novel and his earlier works, 'the philosophical essence of *Bereg* makes the novel distinctly different from the rest of Bondarev's "purely war" prose.'[30] Thus it seems that the appearance of *Bereg* could be viewed as a further step in the development of the conventional Soviet war prose in general, and in the evolution of Bondarev's art in particular.

This brief analysis of the development of recent Soviet war prose, as exemplified in the works of Bykov and Bondarev, makes it possible to identify a number of new traits in the war literature of the last decade. The most significant of these has been a re-evaluation of past events and old, inflexible values. This has been prompted, to a degree, by a new perception of the past and by an attempt to re-assess life today in the light of sacrifices made during the war. This had led in turn to a literary trend in which war events are unified with present-day reality. The behaviour and actions of former soldiers and officers are followed through several decades after the end of the war, and the reactions to past events by representatives of different generations are juxtaposed. Perhaps this process will ultimately transform war prose into purely historical literature in which imaginative fiction will replace the autobiographical element still present in today's war literature.

While these generals trends are characteristic of both Bykov and Bondarev, there is an obvious distinction in the nature of their art. Bykov is concerned in his works mainly with justice and with the fate of the underdog. His attention is always devoted to an area limited in scope, and to the immediate concerns of his protagonists. Bondarev, however, is concerned with the general mechanics of warfare and with the fate of soldiers and generals alike. Bondarev limits himself to the depiction of events taking place on the main front line with Nazi Germany, while Bykov examines in addition the life and struggle of those who were abandoned by the Soviet army and who remained in the territories occupied by the Germans.

The two men employ different artistic techniques. Bykov concentrates on precise imagery, lyricism, and mutual and reciprocal honesty, while Bondarev draws a broad canvas of historical and military events in which characterization suffers at the expense of the more general political, ideological, and historical objectives. Neither Bykov nor Bondarev criticizes the Soviet system or questions its general policies at war or in peace. However, the situations they present and the problems they pose challenge at times the existing order and raise questions to which 'the system' has as yet no answers in sight.

The evolution of the war prose of Bykov and Bondarev in the last decade indicates that while their work shares a common adherence to general patterns of literary development, both writers reach their artistic objectives in different ways and each executes his creative designs in a manner peculiar to his talents. A comparison of their creative work serves as a good example of the range of artistic diversity possible within an aesthetic system which still requires a large degree of ideological and political homogeneity.

4 ❖ Sergei Zalygin: Innovation and variety

Sergei Zalygin belongs to the older generation of Soviet writers. He was born in December 1913, in the village of Durasovka, now in the Soviet Bashkir republic, a part of the Ural region. His father was exiled there from the Tambov district in central Russia, for revolutionary activity. In 1920 the family moved to the city of Barnaul in Siberia. There Zalygin received his elementary education, and later graduated from an agricultural *tekhnikum* (a specialized secondary school). Zalygin had ample opportunity, at an early age, to make practical use of the education and skill he had acquired at school. At the age of sixteen, he was a laboratory assistant at the Barnaul *tekhnikum*; at seventeen he was an official representative of the authorities (*upolnomochennyi*) in the village of Bel'mesovo; and at eighteen, after graduation from the *tekhnikum*, he was delegated to the countryside to work in the capacity of an agronomist.[1]

After a while, Zalygin moved to the city of Omsk in Siberia and enrolled at the hydro-land-reclamation faculty of the Omsk Agricultural Institute. He graduated in 1939 as a qualified engineer hydrologist, and in 1942 he was mobilized and sent to work as a hydrologist in the far north of western Siberia. After the war Zalygin continued to work and study, and in 1948 he defended a dissertation for the academic degree of Candidate of Technical Sciences and became the head of the Agricultural Land-Reclamation Department of the institute from which he initially graduated. In 1955 Zalygin moved to the city of Novosibirsk to assume new duties with the Academy of Sciences. He took leave of absence, however, to write a book, and he never returned to full-time work in his profession. Literature became his main occupation. Zalygin continued to live for a while in Siberia and in the late sixties he finally moved to Moscow, where he now resides. According to Zalygin's own admission, he tries hard to keep in touch with his old profession, but he claims that science develops so swiftly that it is almost impossible to keep up with it.[2]

To many Soviet readers and critics, despite his advanced age, Zalygin is still a young writer. Indeed, he became well known only in the sixties when his major and most important works began to appear. Zalygin, however, began to write at an early age. Literature was always his second love. While still at school he wrote a play which was performed by his schoolmates. His first stories began to appear in 1935, and his first collection of stories, which reflected his experience in the Siberian countryside, was published in 1941 in the city of Omsk. The next collection, *Severnye rasskazy* (Stories of the North), is a reflection of the writer's fascination with the north, and appeared in 1947, also in Omsk. This new collection attracted the attention of the Moscow literary establishment and in February 1949 Zalygin was invited to come to Moscow for a discussion of his creative work. As a result of this encounter Zalygin was recommended for admission to the Writers Union.

Zalygin's talent matured slowly and his early stories are artistically inferior to his later works. The emphasis in the early stories is on description rather than on analysis. We often witness in them a simplistic treatment of character and a reluctance to investigate the motivations of characters. These works are important thematically, however, because one can detect a connection between Zalygin's early stories and his later works. A number of the heroes in Zalygin's mature works are a development of the protagonists first encountered in his early stories.

In the 1940s Zalygin's prose was mainly of local, Siberian, significance. The fifties marked the writer's arrival on the 'all-union' literary scene. In 1952 Valentin Ovechkin's 'Raionnye budni' (District Weekdays) began to appear in *Pravda* (The Truth), giving in a way the necessary impetus for the development of the 'village prose,' which flowered in the decade after Stalin. Zalygin was at that time one of Ovechkin's followers and he did not fail to acknowledge his indebtedness to his teacher.[3] In the spring of 1954, Zalygin spent much of his time on travel in the Siberian countryside, and this resulted in the creation of his sketches depicting life in the Siberian village, a collection entitled 'Vesnoi nyneshnego goda' (In the Spring of this Year), which was subsequently published in *Novyi mir*.[4]

As opposed to most other representatives of 'village prose,' Zalygin's interest was not limited strictly to the investigation and discussion of the life of the countryside in the immediate post-war period. As a scientist and scholar, Zalygin moved in academic circles and was a member of the Soviet intellectual elite, and he used the practical experience gained in his profession for his creative work. His next major work, 'Svideteli' (Witnesses) (1956),[5] is a satirical *povest'*. The main protagonist is Evgen'ia Merkur'evna Arzamasskaia, a lecturer of English in a provincial institute, who returns to her native city to seek witnesses who could certify that she graduated from the local secondary school. While she looks for witnesses to confirm her past she herself observes the lives of her past acquaintances and she realizes that they have all changed for the worse. Three encounters are depicted in which the ethics of different segments of society are portrayed: the family, the realm of higher education and scholarship, and the business world.

'Svideteli' is a satire on the unpleasant phenomena of Soviet life; it dwells on the shortcomings of society and the weaknesses of men and the picture of reality presented in the story is indeed discouraging. The message which emanates from the three encounters is one of man's egotism, greed, and hypocrisy. Most of the characters depicted, regardless of their station in life, are self-centred individuals who care only for their own well-being which is to be attained at any price. Concern for others and for the public cause are empty phrases.

Evgen'ia Merkur'evna appears in the role of the champion of truth and she attempts to teach others. She claims that 'there is only one truth ... It requires that it be served and trusted. And a lie ... has many faces. You can select any one of them and serve it ...'[6] And yet Evgen'ia Merkur'evna herself is not perfect. She wants to teach others how to live but she has her own faults and weaknesses. She wants to help arrange the lives of others while her own life is in a mess. In addition, as one can judge from her past, she has not always adhered to the lofty ethical principles by which she judges others. Thus it appears that both the accusers and the accused, the judges and the judged, have their own shortcomings and imperfections, and they should look first at themselves before pointing at others.

'Svideteli' has shortcomings. There is no stylistic unity in the narrative. Most characters, including the heroine, are sketched only episodically. Yet this work is important for the development of Soviet literature in the immediate post-Stalin period as well as for the evolution of the artistic talent of Zalygin. First of all, 'Svideteli' is a shattering attack on the new brand of philistinism practiced by the middle and upper strata of Soviet society. In addition, it points to the fact that each human being is different, and that man is essentially an imperfect creature. This is an important message which permeates Zalygin's later works: a proposition that the search for truth is often a futile process because many people dwell on the shortcomings of others, turning, at the same time, a blind eye to their own imperfections.

Zalygin's first novel, *Tropy Altaia* (The Altai Paths 1962)[7] is an investigation of the ethics of the community of Soviet scholars. The writer explores the everyday concerns of a group of biologists and geographers on an expedition into the Altai mountains. He juxtaposes those who are concerned with true scholarship with those who are vain and unscrupulous and who use ostensibly scholarly pursuit as a means for the gratification of their own pride. One of the main conflicts in the novel is between the leader of the expedition, Professor Vershinin, and his son, the young student Andrei. The first dreams about a promotion which is to be granted on the basis of illusory scholarly achievements, while the latter, as yet uncorrupted by the pressures of everyday life, makes a real discovery which does not, however, receive the attention it deserves because it conflicts with the scholarly objectives contrived by his father.

Another important theme in the novel is that of man's relationship to nature. The preservation of nature, and, in particular, the conserving of the vast natural resources of Siberia, are one of the writer's essential concerns. Zalygin explores in *Tropy Altaia* man's interaction with nature, and he endeavours to illustrate how nature can in turn affect man. Most of the positive characters are close to nature and they respect it. Their closeness to nature enobles them and separates them, in turn, from those who are indifferent to the environment, and who are out to exploit it for their own benefit. Zalygin's understanding of nature is expressed in his proposition that nothing is identical in our environment; that while there are parallels and interactions between the different components and phenomena of the natural world, each thing and each relationship are different, even unique, and difficult to repeat or recreate.

Artistically *Tropy Altaia* falls short of being a great novel. The work lacks dramatic intensity and artistic or stylistic unity. A number of digressions and sub-plots burden the flow of the narrative. Characterization is inadequate and the epilogue is inconclusive. The novel, however, discusses two issues relatively untouched until recently in Soviet literature: ecology and man's relationship to his natural environment. It also tests the ethical foundations of that scholarship which is directly concerned with the relationship of man to nature.

The 1960s were the years when Zalygin's talent reached its highest peak and when he gained recognition on the 'all-union' literary scene, becoming one of the leading Soviet writers.[8] It is interesting to note, however, that Zalygin reaches artistic excellence not in the works depicting his own milieu, the life of Soviet scholars and the intelligentsia of which he is a part, but rather in the works in which he investigates the fate of the Russian peasant in the period of civil war and collectivization in post-revolutionary Russia. The most important works of this period are 'Na Irtyshe' (By the Irtysh) (1964)[9] and *Solenaia Pad'* (Salt Valley) (1967).[10] In 'Na Irtyshe' Zalygin offers new insights into the process of collectivization in Russia, while in *Solenaia Pad'* he investigates the internal contradictions plaguing the revolutionary forces in the civil war. Both works are set in Siberia, and whereas the masses and popular movements from the background of the plots, at the centre are the fates of individuals. Thus, though Zalygin describes events in his works, man is his main subject. He realizes that men are often helpless in the face of historical events of great magnitude, but his main protagonists refuse to become tools of blind fate. They endeavour to make a choice; they attempt to rationalize their actions, remaining at the same time true to themselves and to their ideas.[11] Most of the heroes in Zalygin's major works are reflective people. They think about life in general and their personal fates in particular. Events in Zalygin's works are not ends in themselves but rather spurs to the evaluation of attitudes toward the social and natural phenomena which form our immediate environment.

The events described in 'Na Irtyshe' take place in March 1931, in the Siberian village of Krutye Luki. The story covers four days in the life of the main protagonist, the *seredniak* (middle peasant), Stepan Chauzov. Stepan is a hardworking man with a strong sense of justice, and he is devoted to his family. He joins the newly formed *kolkhoz* and works hard on its behalf, but he refuses to give voluntarily his grain to the *kolkhoz* sowing fund. He feels that his first responsibility is to his family. Chauzov does not submit to the unjustified demands of Koriakin, the chairman of the *troika* in charge of unmasking the *kulaks*, and he is exiled from his native village. Chauzov is the embodiment of the best qualities of the Russian peasant. Koriakin, on the other hand, is the representative and prisoner of an idea. He is blinded by his own beliefs which have taken complete hold of him. He is no longer the master of the idea, but its slave.

The conflict and contradictions between Chauzov and Koriakin are further developed in *Solenaia Pad'*. In 'Na Irtyshe' the protagonists appear to be political opponents, while in *Solenaia Pad'* the conflict is between members of the same camp. Both the commander of the partisans, Meshcheriakov, and Brusenkov, the Head of the General Revolutionary Staff of the Liberated Territory, appear to be dedicated to the final victory of the revolution; yet they are mortal enemies. Meshcheriakov is portrayed as a human being with virtues and faults, who serves the cause as well as his people with dedication. Brusenkov, on the other hand, is a tyrant and bully. He identifies himself with the cause of the revolution, but since, according to him, his ideals are without fault, he considers himself above criticism. People like Koriakin and Brusenkov act in the name of an allegedly perfect idea and therefore are not selective in the methods used in achieving their goals. According to them the end justifies any means.

The action in *Solenaia Pad'* takes place in the fall of 1919. Siberia is engulfed in the turmoil of civil war. Most people are involved in events the significance of which they cannot fathom. They try to rationalize their actions but are swept away by the tide of events. The sensation of social discord and of the instability of human fate is enhanced in the novel by the shifting use of different images and, in particular, by the protrayal of instability in natural phenomena and changes in the natural environment.

Artistically, 'Na Irtyshe' is Zalygin's best work, unsurpassed as yet by his later novels and stories. In it, Zalygin succeeds in rendering convincingly the essence of the main conflict as well as the spirit of the time. There is complete stylistic and artistic unity in the narrative. There are no unnecessary digressions, nor is there any interference with the natural flow of the narrative. Everything is moved by the artistic images, the author remaining all the time to one side. Each expresses himself in his own highly individual manner, and the author adapts his prose to suit the speech of his protagonists.

Both 'Na Irtyshe' and *Solenaia Pad'* are often viewed by the reading public as attempts to re-interpret history. The first work challenges the pattern previously accepted in Soviet literature of depicting the process of collectivization (as presented, for instance, in works such as Mikhail Sholokhov's *Podniataia tselina* (Virgin Soil Upturned). The second debunks the accepted notion that the revolutionary movement was a homogeneous force. This is one of the reasons for the sharp criticism of Zalygin's treatment of characters such as Chauzov and Brusenkov.

While most Soviet critics praise the artistic qualities of the works discussed, many do not fail to attack Zalygin's conception of the past which, according to them, is not a true reflection of the events taking place in those days. L. Terakopian counteracts such opinions by suggesting that 'each epoch adds new shades to what has already been depicted before; it discovers also new, previously overlooked or insufficiently emphasized, aspects of history.'[12] Indeed, it seems to me, there is no need to rewrite history: indeed, how could one improve on a historical picture of reality which has been presented truthfully and completely in the first place? Zalygin does not re-interpret history. Instead he adds a new dimension to its protrayal, a new link in the artistic re-creation of the past, one which has been missing from the total picture.

The realities of the post-Stalin era have made possible a new approach to the treatment of remote historical events, the novel interpretation of which cannot affect the present situation in Soviet arts and society the way it would have several decades ago. Zalygin did not fail to make use of this opportunity and achieved two important objectives at the same time. He created works of literature of considerable merit; and through his innovative approach to the treatment of the past he helped the Soviet reader fill in a gap in his conception of Russia's history.

Zalygin's creative path can be divided into three distinct periods. The first, of his early artistic experimentation and quest, ended in the mid-fifties with his appearance on the Soviet literary scene and his decision to give up scientific and scholarly pursuits to become a professional writer. The second, of his rapid artistic maturation, ended with the publication of *Solenaia Pad'*, for which Zalygin was awarded the 1968 State Prize for Literature. Zalygin's creative output of the sixties consolidated his position in Soviet literature, and his work in the next decade already bears the mark of a confident and self-assured writer.

The third period is again one of experimentation, with the author treating a variety of new themes and genres. Many writers find certain themes or modes of artistic expression which suit their talents, and concentrate on one particular area of artistic pursuit. Zalygin, however, likes to write on different topics and to work in different genres. Otherwise, he claims, work soon becomes boring and clichés begin to replace true artistic creation. Thus, in the decade following *Solenaia Pad'*, Zalygin has written an autobiographical sketch, literary criticism devoted to nineteenth- and twentieth-century Russian writers and poets, short stories, a 'fantastic' narrative, and two novels so different from each other that the uninitiated reader would hardly believe they were written by the same author.

Zalygin's short stories defy classification. The four stories which appear in the early seventies are all different. They are usually based on events taken from his personal experience. Most of the stories, however, have an invisible connection with the general concerns which permeate the writer's major works. In 'Miatlik lugovoi' (A Meadow Flower) (1971) Zalygin returns to man's relation to nature, to the problem of the uniqueness of each natural creature. In 'Korovii vek' (The Lifetime of a Cow) (1972) Zalygin tries to trace the biological course of the life of a cow and to convey her perception of time. 'Angel'skaia noch'' (The Angelic Night) (1972) is a story in which the distinction between reality and fantasy is almost lost. The hero, a small boy, contemplates all day a meeting with angels, until finally in the night they come to visit him in his dream. In 'Sannyi put'' (On a Sledge in the Forest) (1972) a film director travels in the winter across the *taiga* along the route the heroes of his film are to follow. He wants to see the path with their eyes. He wants to see the surroundings the way they will, but instead he recalls his own past. He cannot get into the required frame of mind for artistic thinking: one cannot force oneself into a creative mood. Zalygin's stories of the seventies have deep meaning. Problems of man and nature, life and death, time and space, the rational and the irrational in man are at the root of his short prose. He investigates these problems further in his later works.

Zalygin returned to the novel in 1973. *Iuzhno-amerikanskii variant*,[13] however, is different from all he had written before. After having read it, one critic even exclaimed: 'I read it and I did not believe my eyes! Has it really been written by Zalygin?'[14] The heroine of the novel is a forty-five-year-old woman and an engineer by profession, Irina Viktorovna Mansurova. She is married to a successful Soviet official and has a teenage son. She is in charge of the department of scientific and research information of a large scientific research institute. As it turns out, Irina Viktorovna is unhappy with her personal life. She feels that life is passing by while she has not as yet lived up to her own expectations. Her husband is not essentially a bad man, but he is in no position to satisfy her desires. Irina often becomes frustrated and depressed, uncertain of her future.

And then, all of a sudden, at a New Year's Eve celebration, Irina makes a resolution and raises a toast for a new love. This resolution leads to an affair with Dr Nikandrov, a married man and a senior official in the institute. This secret relationship lasts for quite a while until Nikandrov, having realized that it is going too far and that it could harm his personal image and his family life, leaves town on a business trip for an extended period of time, without even notifying Irina. Irina Viktorovna is heart-broken and decides to hate Nikandrov.

She needs someone to love, however, and to be loved in turn, and she begins to live in a dream. She creates in her imagination a knight with whom she is in love. The knight is in essence the image of a man whom she encountered once, in the distant past, while travelling to meet her husband-to-be, Mansurov. This man was on his way to an assignment in South America; he proposed to the young Irina and suggested that she should come along with him abroad. As it turned out, the man in whose image the knight was created had died recently, and in the end, Irina remains alone. Nikandrov abandons her and she learns about the knight's death which destroys her dream and her fantasy.

Under close scrutiny there is nothing new or unusual in Zalygin's latest work. Family life and infidelity have been from time immemorial one of the main subjects of literature. In addition, Zalygin's concern with the fate of the family, and, in particular, with the position of the woman in a changing society, is not a new one. In one of his articles, written in the early sixties,[15] Zalygin claims that in the past the woman has been chiefly a family creature. She has been more conservative than man and the transformation of society today, which forces the woman out from the family circle and into the social sphere, affects her stability and has in many cases a traumatic affect on her development as a human being. Zalygin asserts that woman, with all her complexity and inner contradictions, is one of the main subjects of literature and that the time is now ripe for the creation of a present-day *Anna Karenina* which would reflect the burning social and family problems of our times.

There is no question in anyone's mind that *Iuzhno-amerikanskii variant* does not measure up to the artistic level of Tolstoy's classic. But there is a great deal of similarity between the problems of both heroines. Both Irina Mansurova and Anna Karenina live in relative material abundance, and yet both rebel and forsake their peaceful home life for a future full of uncertainty. This rebellion and the quest for a new spirituality are based on an ethical rejection of living a lie. Both have become prisoners in their own homes, enslaved by circumstances, and hypocrites by habit.

Anna is of course younger, and passionate love in the main impulse for her rebellion. Irina Mansurova is older, and she is forced into rebellion by the realization of her own lack of fulfilment as a woman. She senses that life is passing her by, that something has to be done immediately to save the future and retrieve whatever is possible from the past. The most important distinction between Karenina and Mansurova is that they live in different times and in different social conditions. Society judges the two women using different codes of values.

The appearance of Zalygin's new novel had strong repercussions in Soviet literary criticism. Instead of approaching Mansurova as a woman subject to inner biological and psychic processes, characteristic of most women of her age, and trying to understand her unhappiness in this context, most Soviet critics view the novel and the behaviour of the main protagonist as a reflection of Soviet reality. While most critics censure Zalygin in a mild and polite tone, some unleash a virulent attack against the writer, and criticize him in a style reminiscent of the famous Soviet feuilletons of the Stalin era. Thus, for example, Iurii Idashkin identifies the negative ideas and actions of the protagonists with those of the author, and he claims that Zalygin creates images 'which reflect the author's notions about the Soviet intelligentsia, but which are far from logic and reality.'[16]

Iuzhno-amerikanskii variant is discussed by many Soviet critics in the context of the general debate of the early seventies on the relative merits of the *byt* literature of city life. The fate of the liberated Soviet woman is at the root of many such works. But *Iuzhno-amerikanskii variant* poses the problem in a manner much more profound than do most similar works. In most *byt* works the emphasis is on external description, while in Zalygin's novel the stress is on internal analysis. Mansurova searches for an internal equilibrium. She has no argument with her husband, she even feels guilty before him; but she is also unhappy with herself. She lacks the internal harmony and stability which could only be supplied by an inner contentment based on the satisfaction of all material and spiritual needs.

Most negative criticism directed at *Iuzhno-amerikanskii variant* is generated primarily by the bleak picture of Soviet reality which forms the background of this drama. There are few happy families in the novel. The attitude of most characters to their work is at best pragmatic, and their approach to life in general is hypocritical and based on two sets of moral standards: one applicable to oneself and the other one to society in general. Zalygin claims that he usually does not react to criticism and yet he was impelled to reply in print to those who, according to him, attacked him with no good reason.[17] Zalygin defends his use of fantasy in the novel as a literary device. He claims that literature without fantasy is unthinkable.[18]

Zalygin favours the description of the irrational in the human mind because he regards it as a part of real life. He considers himself true to the realism of the nineteenth century and he claims that by virtue of its emphasis on the negative aspects of life, Soviet literature now comes closer to the traditions of classical literature. Zalygin agrees that many characters and, in particular, the scholars in *Iuzhno-amerikanskii variant* are not perfect, but he says that they have their virtues and shortcomings, all that makes them real and human. According to Zalygin, no one is perfect, but everyone has a place in life. Zalygin concedes that it is difficult to create a positive hero. He says that real heroes are created by circumstances, while conditions in the Soviet Union today are not conducive to true heroism.

But if *Iuzhno-amerikanskii variant* is a novel with some clearly defined elements of fantasy (a fantasy which has its foundation in real life), Zalygin's next work

'Os'ka – smeshnoi mal'chik' (Os'ka the Funny Boy) (1973),[19] which has a subtitle 'A fantastic narrative in two periods,' can be regarded as a fantasy for its own sake. In an introduction to this narrative Zalygin tries to explain his attitude to fantasy, and he writes that he arrived at a conclusion that 'each fantasy ought to be restored to the source from which it derives, i.e. to real life. If the circle closes, one can expect some order and logical conclusion, as opposed to a straight line which inevitably leads Nowhere. It appears that I have reached the point where fantasy exists for its own sake.'[20]

Indeed, although there are several real heroes in the narrative, it is very difficult to work out what really happens and what is only in the mind of the main protagonist, Aleksei Drozdov. In the first part he is a young man observing meteorological and natural phenomena in the far north, while in the second part, many years later, he is a professor and doctor of sciences. In his youth, when he is left all by himself, he usually gives himself up to day-dreaming. In the second part, when he is ill, it is difficult to make a distinction between his conscious and subconscious levels of thinking. Certain dreams and recollections are based on past experiences, while others are rooted in fantasy and have no real foundation whatsoever. Such are Drozdov's discussions with the so-called Integral or with the Cockroach, both figments of his imagination.

Zalygin is a scientist as is Drozdov, and the author often works here with language and formulations difficult for the ordinary layman to understand. 'Os'ka – smeshnoi mal'chik' is a work which verges on science fiction. It could be approached as an investigation of the subconscious and its effect on conscious thought. In the first part, fantasy can be seen as a refuge from loneliness. Drozdov is a recluse in the north; he is left there all by himself to observe nature. The mature Drozdov endeavours to solve in fantasy problems to which real-life solutions are out of reach. He lives, apparently, in a world which gives him little satisfaction and from which he is alienated; and he creates, therefore, in his fantasy, the image of another world which could satisfy his intellectual and spiritual needs.

'Os'ka – smeshnoi mal'chik' is a puzzling but interesting work; yet Soviet literary criticism greeted it with almost complete silence. Zalygin probably anticipated such an outcome, for he concluded his introduction to the narrative by saying that he is a convinced realist and will never again return to this unusual genre.

In his next novel, *Komissiia* (1975),[21] Zalygin returns to the theme with which he has been most successful in the past. He investigates the fate of Russian peasants in the civil-war period in a remote village in Siberia. The title of the novel refers to a commission, composed of residents of the village of Lebiazhka, the task of which is to protect the surrounding forests from poachers and thieves in this turbulent period. Although the commission is composed of peasants representing the residents of only one village, each of them exhibits a different way of thinking, and each of them has a different approach to life. The commission appears to act for the good of the people, but each member has a different notion of good and evil, and of how the common good is to be achieved.

The main character of the novel is Nikolai Ustinov. He is a wise and hard-working man with a strong sense of duty and justice. He is against unnecessary bloodshed, and is for mutual understanding between people. Ustinov does not want to take sides in the quarrels and arguments between different factions; he seeks reconciliation. He wants to remain true to himself and to maintain his own course of action which is based on reason and mutual respect. He lives, however, in times of social and political upheavals and he is murdered by an unknown killer. Ustinov's fate indicates that one cannot remain neutral at times of social strife, and that there is no room for a third force when two forces are fighting for life and death.

Another member of the commission, Deriabin, is a dedicated Bolshevik. For him, everyone who opposes the required course of action is a potential enemy and should be removed – by force, if necessary. The conclusion of the novel – a Kolchak detachment arrives in the village and arrests all members of the commission – proves Deriabin correct in his reasoning. Yet he is painted as an inflexible and dogmatic individual who approaches social issues and human relations in a manner in which only one point of view is possible, and in which all must surrender without compromise to the demands of the cause which is allegedly beyond criticism and fault.

Deriabin follows in the steps of Koriakin and Brusenkov; he shares most of their qualities. He is restless and suspicious; he lacks tolerance for the opinions of others. Ustinov, on the other hand, has many traits similar to those characteristic of Chauzov and Meshcheriakov. It is interesting to note that the zeal of Deriabin and Brusenkov is often checked by other people; even in times of civil war this still happens. In 1931, however, Koriakin is an all-powerful despot. He acts in the name of the state and there is no way to check his power.

The only member of the commission who is a simple peasant and represents, in a way, the masses leaves the commission when political and intellectual discussions become its main interest. For the peasant Polovinkin is a practical man, and the long deliberations of the commission appear to him a waste of time. The other members are upset because the depature of Polovinkin could signify that the masses have abandoned them, but Deriabin is unperturbed. He claims that it is necessary to lead the ignorant people despite themselves and even against their will.

In the novel, Zalygin renders perfectly the atmosphere of confusion, instability, and lack of direction which permeated the Russian hinterland in the period of revolution and civil war. He does this, however, not by studying the movement of the masses, but rather by exploring the moods, thoughts, and actions of individual peasants. The period of civil war is a time in which people are forced to make decisions about things they little understand. They are impelled to take sides and to join factions, the objectives of which are very obscure to them.

The Russian peasant mistrusts the outsider and seeks guidance within himself. He is sceptical about the use of political theories and ideologies, and he interprets them as a tool to be used by those who seek to gain uncontrolled power. One peasant in *Solenaia Pad'* suggests that 'power and authority are all the same power and authority, no matter from what side you approach it! It may happen that a *muzhik*, elected by ourselves, will turn out to be a hundred times worse than the emperor the tsar! ... the emperor or a peasant and worker in power are equally interested first of all in their own power, and only later in all the rest in the world.'[22]

Similarly, when Polovinkin decides to leave the commission, he makes the accusation to its members that their deliberations obscure the real issue, which is a hidden desire for power. He claims that to him it makes no difference who rules over him, 'whether it is is the tsar or a peasant-neighbour, I hate and detest them both equally! They are all for themselves, they are people of a particular kind. While all the other people: there are simply too many of them to be noticed.'[23] Thus it appears that to the peasant political ideology is tantamount to power, which he treats with suspicion and mistrust because he knows from personal experience that it can easily be abused.

The main plot of *Komissiia* develops along two distinct lines. On the one hand, the author explores the social aspects of the conflict in which the masses are involved while, on the other hand, he investigates the personal lives and relationships of the leading characters. This is particularly true of Ustinov, a happily married man and a grandfather, who is at the same time passionately loved by another woman, Zinaida. Zinaida, a childless woman with an indifferent husband, prompts Ustinov to abandon his family and to run away with her. In Zinaida's character is expressed the victory of dark passion and the irrational desire for love over the logic of everyday life. Domna, Ustinov's wife, on the other hand, is also a proud woman but she is able to contain her emotions; her reason is in control of her feelings.

The tragic aspect of both the social and the personal elements of the novel blend together in the touching scene in the concluding lines of the narrative. The death of Ustinov does not solve any of the problems causing the turmoil in this remote area, but his death brings peace to the personal strife of the two women struggling for the heart and mind of the same man. At the very time that the members of the commission are being led into the village square to be punished, in another corner of the village Zinaida and Domna, both stricken by grief and forgotten by all, are dragging the coffin with the dead body of the man they love on his last path to eternal peace.

Thematically, *Komissiia* is in many ways similar to *Solenaia Pad'*, and yet it is deeper and more complex. There are in the novel both an underlying idea of man's responsibility for the preservation of nature and of his environment and an invisible link connecting the personal fates of the heroes and the Siberian land with its historical past. The historical background influences and conditions the approach of the peasants to life. Simple peasant wisdom and a belief that in the long run common sense will prevail and a solution will be found to all problems besetting the land characterize the peasants' unhurried approach to the most complex problems of daily life. Despite the victory of the revolution and the removal of the tsar, simple peasants continue to believe in some kind of higher justice; they still have a vision of an idealized future based on ethical principles which transcend local issues and the daily worries of man.

Zalygin achieves his artistic objectives in the novel by a number of means. There is in the novel a constant juxtaposition of the present with the past. Intertwined with the flow of the main narrative are elements of folklore, tales, myths, and the *skaz* (a story told by one of the characters in his own words, making possible the use of colourful and idiosyncratic speech, often in dialect). The language of *Komissiia* is the language of the Siberian peasant. The author seldom digresses; what he wants to say he usually expresses through his heroes.

The appearance of Zalygin's new novel has been hailed in Soviet criticism as one of the significant literary events of the seventies. The critics do not hide their satisfaction that Zalygin returns to the theme and genre in which he has been most successful in the past. One critic praises Zalygin's fresh approach to the treatment of Ustinov, in whose character the author endeavours to combine man's practical attitude to his environment with a spiritual and philosophical understanding of the function of nature.[24] Another sees the strength of the novel in the artistic fusion of the realistic narrative with elements of the parable and of the *zhitie* (hagiography), and in the diversity of symbolic elements taken from poetic lore.[25]

As always in the discussion of Zalygin's treatment of historic events, the question arises whether the writer's novel treatment of the past does not constitute a reappraisal of Soviet history. Do his new insights into the attitude of the Siberian peasants toward change challenge the pattern already established, in Soviet history and literature, for depicting the events of the revolution? Valerii Dement'ev hastens to advise that 'Sergei Zalygin did not endeavour, at any time, to "correct" history,'[26] but he adds that our present perception of the civil war is much more complex than was our understanding of the same events twenty-five years ago. It is suggested that the new approach of Zalygin to the treatment of the civil war is significant because it raises problems which are as relevant today as they were a generation ago.

Indeed, the problems of man's relation to nature and of his ethical values and principles, which are discussed in *Komissiia*, have become important concerns, and have been overlooked for many years in Soviet literature. Zalygin's new novel reminds the reader than problems of justice and morality, of man and his environment, of love and death, are always the concerns of free men. Zalygin's heroes are thinking heroes: they rationalize their actions, they argue and search for new solutions to eternal problems. Chingiz Aitmatov once suggested that 'the struggle of ideas is an eternal and unavoidable one. This struggle is in essence the moving force of social progress.'[27] Zalygin's new approach to the revolution and the civil war, therefore, changes them from static one-dimensional events into controversial and contradictory multi-dimensional phenomena (the results of which are well known, but the process of which is still enigmatic and insufficiently explored).

Zalygin is one of the leading Russian writers, as well as a respected member of the Soviet literary establishment. He is perhaps not an outstanding writer but he is certainly, by any standards, a good writer, particularly when he depicts the history of the Siberian peasants. But Zalygin is also a Soviet writer and man, and he is exposed to all the influences and constraints to which Soviet people and writers are subjected. Thus, on the one hand, Zalygin claims to be tolerant of the views of his heroes and the ideas of his opponents in real life. He claims that ideas are like people and bear the peculiar traits characteristic of men. Since there are no perfect people there are also no perfect ideas, and we should not expect from ideas what we do not expect from people. Therefore, he suggests, we should treat the ideas of others with the same respect and understanding with which we treat people.[28]

On the other hand, however, Zalygin the Soviet citizen is sensitive to the phenomena of daily Soviet life and he does not fail to react to them. On one occasion he attacks American involvement and atrocities in Vietnam, while on another he advocates a problem-solving and socially significant literature.[29] But all this is expressed in his journalistic writings. In his art he creates real people with real problems, most of which were unexplored in Soviet literature. We can conclude by noting that Zalygin's talent began to mature rapidly during the relative relaxation of literary controls after the denunciation of the 'personality cult' of Stalin. The new atmosphere made possible the evolution of his creative talent and made possible his new approach to the treatment of old artistic and historical values.

5 ✤ Valentin Rasputin: Village prose reconsidered

In the late 1960s, when 'village prose' reached its highest point of development, the young Siberian writer Valentin Rasputin was making his first steps into Soviet literature. Now, a decade later, it is possible to say that 'village prose' has lost much of its previous impact as a literary trend while Rasputin continues to create works of art which are close in spirit to the best traditions of the 'village prose' of the sixties.

Rasputin was always regarded as a writer close to the village theme in Soviet literature. His plots are set in remote Siberian villages and his heroes are usually simple peasants. His art, however, is unique, and it is difficult to place it within the mainstream of 'village prose.' Rasputin's protagonists resemble closely those of Fedor Abramov or Vasilii Belov, but their problems and conflicts are of a universal nature and transcend the narrow confines of the remote countryside.

Rasputin was born in 1937 in the Siberian village of Ust'-Uda, on the Angara river, three hundred miles from the city of Irkutsk. His father was a peasant and labourer and served during the war in the army. The young Rasputin managed to get an education and he graduated in 1959 from the faculty of history and philology of the Irkutsk State University.[1] While at university Rasputin worked part-time in a youth newspaper. After graduation he continued his journalistic career, publishing at the same time several collections of sketches based on his journalistic experience.[2]

The year 1967 marked the birth of Rasputin the fiction writer, when he published his first collection of stories *Chelovek s etogo sveta* (A Man from This World)[3] as well as his first novelette 'Den'gi dlia Marii' (Money for Mariia).[4] The appearance of these works marked his emergence on the Soviet literary scene, thus demonstrating that the art of a provincial writer can transcend local confines and becomes relevant to the wider Soviet reading public.

While the art and confidence of Rasputin matured gradually, his artistic gift and the thematic concerns which occupy him today were already evident in his early stories. In stories such as for example 'Rudolfio' and 'Vstrecha' (An Encounter)[5] Rasputin deals with the sensitivity of man and the unpredictability of fate. He investigates the complexity of human nature and points out man's inability to understand his fellow man. He demonstrates vividly in these stories that what might seem to one individual a joke could appear to another person a matter of life and death. Already in his early stories Rasputin displays a keen sense of observation and an ability to understand his characters. He executes his artistic designs with a notable degree of truthfulness and sincerity, a fact which makes his prose believable and artistically convincing.

Rasputin is not a prolific writer. Between 1967 and 1976 he published only four novellas and some short pieces. Yet this has been enough to place him in the foreground of Soviet literature, and to gain for him the recognition which even prominent writers often fail to receive during their lifetime.

The plot of Rasputin's first major work 'Den'gi dlia Marii' is built around a conflict which is common in everyday Soviet life. Mariia, a simple peasant woman, is forced into taking charge of a village store. She does not have the necessary qualifications for this position. She is hardly literate, and when an inspector arrives he discovers that a thousand rubles are missing. He gives her five days to repay the money, or else she will have to face criminal charges. Nothing is changed by the fact that Maria is an honest woman, that she did not steal the money. The law is merciless. This incident is only the starting point for the development of the plot. Mariia is a passive woman and the task of getting the money is left to her husband, the *kolkhoz* driver Kuz'ma. The story begins with Kuz'ma getting ready to go to town to visit his brother, Aleksei, whom he has not seen for seven years, in order to ask him for the money still required. The story ends with Kuz'ma facing the door of his brother's apartment in the city.

The narrative shifts continuously from the depiction of the present to the portrayal of the previous two days which have been spent trying to borrow as much money as possible from fellow villagers. In between we learn about the background of the protagonists and about the history of the village store. Kuz'ma and Mariia are simple people with four children. Both of them work hard. Suddenly an occurrence of extraordinary importance shakes their existence to its very foundations. This situation reveals their relationship to each other, and uncovers the true nature of those to whom they turn for help. Most of the poor and uneducated peasants are more generous than the educated specialists and office workers. The simple people are guided by compassion and a genuine desire to help, rather than by any desire to put on a show of solidarity behind which there is no commitment.

The juxtaposition of the city and the countryside throughout the story emphasizes unfailingly the spiritual superiority of the latter. The important city-dwellers, whom Kuz'ma encounters on the train, look down at the peasants. They consider themselves superior, and they treat Kuz'ma in a condescending manner. One has a feeling that there exists a deep abyss separating the city and its inhabitants from the remote village. In one compartment of the train Kuz'ma meets an old peasant couple who provide a model of a devoted family. The old woman says that 'by their origin all people come from villages ... And human goodness, respect for the elderly and diligence all originate in the countryside.'[6] She prides herself on the fact that she and her husband have been faithful to each other all their lives. She is for strong family ties. She is the opposite of the young man in the same compartment who advocates dissoluteness and infidelity. Kuz'ma says that in the village marriage is a serious matter and not a temporary diversion as often happens in the city. In the countryside a man and a woman come together in order to build a life and to create a future for their children.

It appears that the peasants have little trust in those who have lost their 'roots'; similarly Kuz'ma doubts whether his brother will help him. Mariia, who visited Aleksei several years ago, tells him that it would be better to stay with strangers and that Aleksei would not help them anyway. This perhaps explains Rasputin's reluctance to take us into the city apartment of Kuz'ma's brother. He does not want to disappoint us. We have come by now to appreciate Kuz'ma and his selfless and unfailing dedication to Mariia, and we surely would hate to see the failure and humiliation of our hero.

'Den'gi dlia Marii' caught the eye of Moscow critics not only because of the nature of the conflict in the story, but also because of the quality of its art, which has all the ingredients of true craftsmanship. One notes the writer's unobtrusive manner of narration, in which his voice blends with the voices of the protagonists; the smooth transition from the present to the past; and the use of numerous artistic devices such as flashbacks, dreams, the symbolism of nature, prejudice, simple people's wisdom, fortune-telling. All these contribute to this story.

The first major work by Rasputin to appear in an 'all-union' literary journal was published in 1970, three years after the appearance of 'Den'gi dlia Marii.' His new novelette 'Poslednii srok' (The Final Term)[7] is in many respects similar to 'Den'gi dlia Marii.' It is set in a remote Siberian village; the course of events is highly localized; the action lasts only several days; and, as in the former story, there is a constant juxtaposition and comparison of the values and actions of the inhabitants of the city with those of the villagers. But that is almost all there is in common between the two stories. In 'Den'gi dlia Marii' Kuz'ma is a positive hero; you feel sorry for him, but it is difficult to identify with him. He is not a man of decisive action.

The main protagonist of 'Poslednii srok' is the eighty-year-old peasant woman Anna. The story opens with Anna on her death-bed expecting her approaching demise, and it ends three days later with her death. The old woman is ready to die;

she has no fear and no regrets; she has fulfilled her duty and accepts death as an inevitable conclusion of a long and perhaps even tiresome existence.

Anna's only wish is to see her children and to take leave of them before her final departure. Anna lives with her son Mikhail in her native village. The other children live far away in different towns and cities. All the children, except for the youngest daughter who lives in Kiev, come to the funeral but the old woman refuses to succumb to death. The arrival of the children infuses a new spark of life in her. John Steinbeck once wrote that 'death is a personal matter, arousing sorrow, despair, fervor, a dry-hearted philosophy. Funerals, on the other hand, are social functions.'[8]

Indeed, Anna's death is her personal matter; it does not concern her children who are all wrapped up in their private affairs. The children have gathered to a social function: to do their last duty and to help bury their mother. They become irritated when Anna thinks and speaks in their presence of life and not of death. They tell her that they are happy that her health improves, regretting at the same time that they will have to return again to partake in the funeral at a later time. Anna is in no rush to die, she knows that nature will take its course, while her children are in a rush to live and to get away from the nearness of death as soon as possible. The night the children leave, Anna dies. There was nothing for her to live for anymore.

There are two major themes in the story and the story is narrated on two different planes. On the one hand, there is the depiction of everyday village life, with particular emphasis on the lives of the characters concerned; on the other, there is the psychological investigation of death and the process of dying. Anna is depicted in a state which ranges somewhere between the end of life and the beginning of death. Death is a mystery difficult to fathom, but it is also a prosaic occurrence, particularly in the daily life of those who are not touched by it directly.

Rasputin penetrates deeply into the mind of his heroine. He re-creates her inner world and he contrasts her spirituality and selflessness with the shallowness and lack of ethical principles of her children. Rasputin thinks of all the children as negative characters,[9] yet it appears that those who live farther away from their native village, those who have been removed from their 'roots' earlier, are more hypocritical and self-centred than the others. And for that matter the simple Mikhail, who has taken care of his old mother during all these years, but who cannot wait for his mother to die and drinks most of the vodka prepared for the funeral repast, appears to the reader in a better light than his more sophisticated sister who arrives from the city for the funeral.

It has been suggested that 'home is one of the most important motifs'[10] in Rasputin's works; that Anna represents the very essence and spirit of the home and the family. In the narrative the departure of the children, who leave their mother's nest and their native lands, does not inspire one with much hope for the future of the family in urban society. The children gather for what is supposed to be their mother's funeral but they have nothing in common, nothing to talk about; they are strangers to each other. There thus appears to be a generation gap between the living and the dying, and an environmental gap between those residing close to their 'roots' and to nature and those who have traded, for material well-being and personal comfort, goodness, simplicity, and beauty, which all supposedly originate in the countryside. In the words of one critic 'the main conflict of the story is the conflict between spirituality and the lack of it ... Anna has a soul, while her children have only psychology.'[11]

The merits of 'Poslednii srok' are not limited to the originality of its plot. The power of the story is enhanced by the artistic mastery with which it is executed. Sergei Zalygin says that 'most important for me is the sensation of completeness in this work ... I have learned about the heroes just as much as I was supposed to know about them.'[12] Indeed, Rasputin penetrates deeply into the character of his heroine and depicts in minute detail the last three days of her life, something which is close to the literary tradition of Tolstoi. Yet it is possible to say that he is succinct in depicting his characters: he tells us only what we need to know, only what is relevant for the movement of the plot, leaving out all the unessential detail.

M. Chudakova suggests that Rasputin 'gives his heroine an opportunity to express herself, he listens to her without interrupting or hurrying her ... When one reads the story one cannot rid oneself of the strange sensation that the author is not the "creator" of the language of his heroine but rather her listener, and that he follows together with us her talk.'[13] The voice of the narrator blends in the story with the voices of his heroes while the narrator himself remains on the side lines. There are no unnecessary digressions and no moralizing. The author does not pass judgment on the actions of his heroes, nor does he suggest what other course of action they could adopt. Rasputin is a dispassionate observer who re-creates the world of his protagonists without interfering with the course of their lives.

For his next significant work Rasputin's admirers had to wait another four years, but the writer did not disappoint them. The main heroine of Rasputin's new story 'Zhivi i pomni' (1974)[14] is the young woman Nastena, the wife of the deserter Andrei Gus'kov who hides himself in the forest next to the Angara river. This is not to say that the nature of the conflict in the story is completely new to Soviet literature. In 1957 Chingiz Aitmatov published a story 'Litsom k litsu'[15] in which the wife of a deserter denounced her husband to the authorities. Rasputin avoids such a simplistic solution; instead, it is Nastena who takes upon herself the guilt of her husband and pays for it dearly with her own life and with the life of her unborn child.

'Zhivi i pomni' begins with the disappearance of an axe in the Gus'kov's bath-house. It is a bad omen. It symbolizes the impending terrible conclusion of the story. Nastena senses with her heart that her husband is somewhere around and it is not long before she encounters him. Andrei confides in her but even his old parents, with whom Nastena resides, are not to learn his hiding place. Andrei lives in the forest far from human sight. A wolf begins to visit him and Andrei learns how to howl. Little by little Andrei becomes himself like an animal. He lives only by instinct. The only force that guides him is the desire to survive at any price. Weakness and cowardice are his driving forces.

The real heroine of the story is Nastena. Her devotion to her husband is unquestionable. He is the only man in her life. She knows that what she is doing is wrong but she considers herself guilty along with her husband. She is sure that he has come home to see *her*; that he deserted in order to save himself for *her*. She overestimates, of course, her husband's dedication to his family. He was unfaithful to her on numerous occasions. In the past he has treated her badly. He was angry that she could not bear him a child. Now, when the end of the war is already in sight he wants to save his life at any cost.

Nastena takes on a heavy burden too difficult for her to carry. Little by little she is driven into a dead end and into desperation. Her pregnant belly begins to show; the fellow villagers begin to suspect that Andrei is somewhere around; and finally, when she is pursued while in a boat on the way to see her husband, she jumps into the Angara and takes along her unborn child. The act of Nastena is perhaps irrational and it runs counter to human logic, but she is driven to it by the dark force of fate which she could not overcome. The tragedy of Nastena is enhanced by the fact that she desired so much to live; that she wanted so much to be happy. She trusted life but she was subdued by the elements. According to the letter of the law Nastena is guilty. Hiding a deserter is a grave crime, but the author is compassionate to his heroine and he asks that she be forgiven: such is the tone of the narrative.

As in his previous works, Rasputin succeeds in this story in penetrating the spiritual world of his heroes. He contrasts the meanness, cowardice, and egotism of Andrei with the selflessness, devotion, and goodness of Nastena. He also contrasts the characteristic qualities of his heroes with the arriving spring. There is a sensation of pureness and renewal in the air. The Angara is set free from the winter ice. Nature comes to life while our heroes are doomed to death, be it physical or spiritual. The narrative includes a whole range of artistic devices. Premonitions, omens, dreams, and the symbolism of nature are all widely used in the story. The intensity of narration grows steadily and it leads finally to a tragic climax which is realistic and believable.

The three major works by Rasputin discussed so far are set in remote villages and the main protagonists are peasants. These stories, however, transcend the confines of the countryside because they deal with conflicts and problems which are eternal. Life and death, goodness and evil, family and loneliness, crime and duty, are topics which have no bounds in time or space. Rasputin's latest novelette 'Proshchanie s Materoi' (Parting with Matera) (1976)[16] is different. There are many similarities with his earlier works, but the spirit of the story is different. Its message is on the surface, and the parallels with the 'village prose' of the 1960s are there for all to see.[17] The main subject of this new story is the ethical implications of the ruthless modernization to which the countryside is exposed, a process which often takes place against the wishes of the peasants who are the main victims of the intrusion of so-called civilization and technological progress.

In 1972 Rasputin published a short story 'Vniz i vverkh po techeniu' (Up and Down the River),[18] to which critics paid little attention at the time, but which occupies an important place in Rasputin's work. Now when one reads the later 'Proshchanie s Materoi,' one can easily see that the idea of this new story was contained in a nutshell in 'Vniz i vverkh po techeniu.' We encounter in the latter a young writer, Viktor, who goes to his native village to visit his parents. When he arrives there he realizes, however, that the village he knew in his childhood has been destroyed and covered with water to make room for an artificial lake for a new hydroelectric station.

There is no glorification of the past in 'Vniz i vverkh po techeniu,' just a nostalgia for it. On his way to see his parents the young writer thinks about his childhood and about his native village; about the effects of technological progress on the way of life of the local people; and about how elusive and difficult to comprehend real happiness is. Viktor becomes depressed in the new settlement of his parents. He begins to realize that he used to have something to lean on: his birth place, the memories of his childhood, and the traditions associated with his home. Now all this is gone. It has been swept away by the winds of industrialization. Before, in his native village, happiness was associated with spiritual qualities, while now, in the new settlement, happiness is measured in terms of money.

The intensity of narration in the story begins to grow with Viktor's expectations when he starts out on his trip to the village. These expectations, however, never materialize. He intends to spend several months there, but he can hardly stay there that many days. His visit to the new village has an anticlimactic effect on Viktor, and we know almost nothing about his trip back to town. The story is an account of a dream destroyed by the realities of everyday life. Now a new dream, based on this new reality, will have to be created.

In 'Proshchanie s Materoi' the conflict is similar but instead of being told by an outsider about the fate of the village and its inhabitants, the drama is acted out for us by the artistic images created by the author. And if 'Vniz i vverkh po techeniu' is a traveller's sketch, 'Proshchanie s Materoi' is a mature work of art.

The main subject of 'Proshchanie s Materoi' is the fate of the 300-year-old village Matera, located on a remote island on the Angara river. The village is doomed to destruction in order to make room for the waters of a man-made sea which is to be part of a huge new hydroelectric-project. The author renders an account of the last summer of the island as it is perceived by the old woman Dar'ia who, together with several other old women, refuses to leave the island until the very last day of its existence. The story focuses on the monumental problems facing society, and questions the ethical foundations of human progress. Rasputin has recently voiced an opinion that 'now, as never before, should be posed the question of the scholar's moral right to make a scientific discovery.'[19] Industrialization and technological progress are advancing rapidly into regions as yet untouched by man, allegedly with the sole purpose of bettering the lives of the people concerned. Yet this is being done against the wishes of those whose lives are affected most by these changes. The question remains: what is really good for man and who is to decide it? What is the relationship of the present to the past, and how much of the past should one be prepared to sacrifice in order to build a future of which the advantages are, perhaps, only illusory?

It is suggested that the name of the village, Matera, relates to the Russian *mat'* (mother) and to the Russian conception of the holiness of mother-earth.[20] The name alludes also to the concept that nature has not been created by man and, therefore, that man has no right to tamper with it. The impending flooding of Matera could be compared to a great calamity, to a universal flood, the end of our world, because that is how the main protagonists of the story perceive the forthcoming events. All their past is connected with the village; all their relatives are buried here, while the future holds nothing in store for them. One of the old men who moved to the new settlement ahead of time died soon after his departure. He disintegrated mentally; the change was too much for him. The younger people are ready, some are even eager, for a change; but they are inexperienced, and they have invested little in the past of Matera, while Dar'ia's son, Pavel, who is a foreman in the *kolkhoz*, asks himself: 'Is the price to be paid for the change not too high?'[21]

The old Dar'ia represents the values of the past, its ethics and traditions. She feels sorry for man today because, according to her, he is a weak creature while life and nature are powerful. Pavel's son, Andrei, tells her that now people have machines, that man has conquered nature, to which Dar'ia replies that man has become the slave of the machine and that the pace of life is such that it will destroy man. Dar'ia is sorry for man because, according to her, man often acts against himself. It appears that there is an inner irrational force which drives man and he often acts unconsciously against his own interests. Dar'ia says that God is in everyone, even in those who do not believe in Him, and that man must have a soul (*dusha*).

It is not difficult to see, from the tenor of the narrative and from Rasputin's statements in regard to his work, that he identifies with Dar'ia and with many of her ideals. Symbolically, nature in the story is stronger than man and it emerges victorious in the struggle with encroaching progress. The removal of the old women from the island is not shown. The people who are supposed to transport them to the new settlement lose their way in the fog. Similarly there is a symbolic scene in which the workers try in vain to destroy an old tree. They cannot cut it down, and they cannot set it on fire, and as long as the tree remains alive Matera will be alive. It is another example that man is weaker than nature and that he has no right to destroy what he has not created himself.

Artistically, in his new story, Rasputin is true to himself. As in most of his other stories the narrator is at one side, not interfering with the flow of the narrative. Different characters can be distinguished by their language, and the more the fate of a given hero is tied up with the past of Matera, the more extensively does he use the local dialect. Symbolic devices are used throughout the story. The impending doom is symbolized by contrasting light and darkness, sun and thunder. Even the sun does not shine in its normal manner. It continues to shine but there is little light and warmth coming from it. There are also elements from Russian folklore in the story, and a *domovoi* (goblin) makes several appearances at the beginning and the conclusion of the story. On numerous occasions Rasputin compares the flow of water with the flow of time. It is impossible to stop the flow of time. Similarly it is impossible to stop the flow of water, and yet man tries to change its course, deluding himself that he can harness the river, control nature, and exploit it without bearing full responsibility and even receiving punishment for what he does.

To enhance the message Rasputin contrasts the people in charge of flooding the island with its old inhabitants. The officials are heartless bureaucrats interested only in the fulfilment of their plan, while the old peasants are concerned with the preservation of their traditions, their memories, and the spiritual values associated with the past. Rasputin shows clearly that official government agencies cannot be trusted with the task of protecting historical and cultural monuments. One house on Matera has been singled out for protection by the Academy of Sciences and it was supposed to be removed intact before the island was to be destroyed. And yet, even despite the fact that a deposit had been paid for it, no one ever claimed it and it was set on fire. Even the name of the head official in charge of the flooding operations is symbolic. His name is Zhuk, in translation 'beetle,' an insect which can destroy nature as well as the very fabric of life.

This brief analysis of Rasputin's most important works makes it clear that while on the surface there are different themes in the major stories, there is an underlying artistic and philosophical unity. The major protagonists in all the stories are simple peasant women. The prototype for Anna is Rasputin's grandmother, while the prototype for Nastena and Dar'ia is the collective image of a Russian woman who is by nature 'good, devoted, selfless, and ready for self-sacrifice; a woman ... who cannot say that I am innocent but you are guilty.'[22] According to Rasputin he values most in the Russian woman her 'goodness, tranquillity, conscientiousness, and the feeling of an involuntary responsibility and guilt for all and everything that happens in this world.'[23]

It is not difficult to detect here the influence of Dostoevskii, an influence and admiration which Rasputin does not conceal.[24] Indeed, this feeling of sharing a common guilt with others is characteristic of many of Rasputin's heroes. Kuz'ma feels guilty for Mariia; Anna feels guilty for her children; Nastena takes upon herself the guilt of Andrei; while Dar'ia feels guilty before her ancestors whom she abandons on Matera. All the important women protagonists in Rasputin's stories are mothers. Mariia, Anna, Dar'ia are real mothers; Nastena is a symbolic mother. In addition, it is possible to say that Matera is the symbol of mother-earth. All women-mothers are compassionate and forgiving, and blame no one for their own suffering. In one of Rasputin's earlier stories, 'Vasilii i Vasilisa' (Vasilii and Vasilisa) (1967),[25] the wife has driven out from the house a husband who almost killed her, but she forgives him when he is on his deathbed.

Among the artistic devices used extensively by Rasputin are dreams and visions, the creation of special natural effects to suit the moods of the characters, the author's peculiar style, and the specific attention he devotes to the use of language. Language is the only aspect of Rasputin's creative work which he plans beforehand. He prepares a little dictionary for each of his characters and he separates them by their mode of speech. At the early stages of his work he distinguishes his protagonists only by their language. He knows how they speak before he knows what they are going to do. Rasputin's style is flexible; his narratives flow smoothly; his language is precise, but it also has a stern poetic quality. He uses the local Siberian dialect extensively, and it is even possible to say that at times the narrator himself falls under the influence of the language of his heroes.

Dreams are an important artistic component in Rasputin's stories. Most of the dreams are symbolic but they relate closely to real life. On the very first page of 'Den'gi dlia Marii,' before his departure to town, Kuz'ma dreams that he knocks on a window and asks for 'den'gi dlia Marii' (money for Mariia). His request is granted; he is given the money. Kuz'ma is still full of hope, he wants to believe that his brother will give him the necessary cash. But the nearer he gets to town the stronger become his doubts. On the train he has another dream in which he sees a general meeting of the *kolkhoz* members. They collect all the money required but it disappears in a mysterious manner, leaving Kuz'ma bewildered and terrified.

In 'Zhivi i pomni' a dream forms the compositional centre of the story. Nastena and Andrei have exactly the same dream while they are thousands of miles apart. In this dream Nastena visits Andrei at the front and urges him to return home. She says she is tired of looking after the children. This dream alludes to the forthcoming meeting of Andrei and Nastena and to her pregnancy.

In 'Proshchanie s Materoi' Dar'ia has a vision in which her parents tell her to prepare properly their house for its final demise. Dar'ia paints and washes the house and grants it the last respects which are usually accorded to a dead man before burial. According to Dar'ia you must respect the place that feeds you and the house that shelters you.

It is possible to sense in all Rasputin's stories a certain dramatic tension; a feeling that time is running out. Perhaps the title 'Poslednii srok' could be applied to all the stories under discussion. Mariia and Kuz'ma are faced with the prospect of jail, and they have only a few days to solve their pressing problems. Anna lives on borrowed time and the arrival of her children only postpones for a few days her inevitable death. Nastena is at an impasse and the day of her reckoning is approaching with increasing rapidity, while Matera is doomed and its old inhabitants are to face inevitable physical and spiritual disintegration. Similarly the title 'Zhivi i pomni' is applicable to all the stories because in each of them there is a hidden message that man should perhaps live differently; that he should learn a lesson and draw conclusions from the past in order not to repeat the mistakes of others.

Nature and the preservation of the environment are constant concerns of Rasputin. He is worried 'about the future fate of the Baikal ... Siberia is unthinkable without the majestic Angara ... The Siberian forests need careful protection and care.'[26] According to Rasputin 'Proshchanie s Materoi' is 'about the changes which take place in present-day Siberia at which I look not with the eyes of an outsider, who comes to conquer and transform this amazing and stern land, but with the eyes of a native inhabitant of Siberia.'[27]

But Rasputin advocates not the preservation of the external environment only. He defends also the internal fabric of life and the spiritual values which are associated with this life and with the environmental atmosphere. And this is precisely the reason why 'Proshchanie s Materoi' is not to the liking of many Soviet critics. Until the appearance of Rasputin's last work, all one could hear in Soviet criticism was praise for the new rising star of Soviet literature. Rasputin kept clear, in his earlier works, from the main stream of the 'village prose' by avoiding the social aspect of village life and by concentrating on the personal dramas of its inhabitants.

'Proshchanie s Materoi' is different. It aims at the very heart of the philosophy of the Soviet state, which is closely associated with urbanization and technological progress. It points clearly at what might appear to be the insurmountable conflict between the individual, who is totally wrapped up in himself, and the impersonal image of the collective state which presumes to have the necessary answers to all questions. It alludes to the facts that life is much more complex than the planners would have us believe and that there are many problems to which there are no readily available solutions. For that matter, although Rasputin raises such problems, he does not propose any solutions to them. All he wants is that his readers should ponder and search for answers both ethical and just. He tells his readers: *zhivi i pomni* – live and remember. Build a future without forgetting your past, remembering that one cannot build happiness on the misfortunes of others.

'Proshchanie s Materoi' has provoked a strong and mixed reaction in Soviet literary criticism. While the critics acknowledge that it is a work of art of considerable artistic merit, they do not fail to point out its ideological shortcomings. Feliks Kuznetsov claims, for example, that Rasputin has reached in this story a certain boundary, a certain limit; that there is no need to carry this argument any further and that life now poses new and different questions which should become the concern of prose writers.[28] O. Salynskii compares Rasputin's earlier works with his last story and he claims that while 'in his previous works Rasputin was able to give a genuine philosophical interpretation of life, in 'Proshchanie s Materoi' the depth of his philosophical conceptions diminishes considerably.'[29]

The truth of the matter is that in 'Proshchanie s Materoi' Rasputin's philosophical ideals are as deep as they have ever been before, but they are also placed in a broader perspective. They hint at personal dramas connected with the deterioration of the quality of man and of life which is associated with what is termed social progress. Rasputin is even criticized for what earned him praise on numerous previous occasions: for identifying with his characters and not interfering with the natural flow of his narratives. It is claimed that 'the author's voice appears to be diluted in the narrative. The author's position merges with the position of his heroine and it becomes quite vulnerable.'[30] What is probably expected from Rasputin is a clear artistic statement as to where he stands in relation to his heroes and the problems discussed; a statement in support of the Soviet way of life which would, however, surely reduce the artistic value of the story.

In 'Proshchanie s Materoi' Rasputin is concerned with the relationship of the present to the past, while little attention is devoted to the future which, according to Dar'ia, is difficult to predict or to foresee. Those responsible for implementing the changes for the future, the people in charge of the flooding operations, are perceived by the reader as individuals who are out to destroy the natural life of Matera and of its past. We do not think of them as 'builders of better times to come.' The official criticism resents such a portrayal of the workers who are in charge of the implementation of official Soviet plans. The critics decry the fact that 'little attention is devoted [in ''Proshchanie s Materoi'] to socially active people,'[31] who are the builders of a new communist society and of a bright future for all.

Rasputin is not concerned in his works with 'positive' or 'negative' heroes. He believes in the image of a man who is alive and who can be trusted. He claims that the reader should not necessarily have to look in a work of art for someone to emulate. It is more important for him that a book should impel the reader to think about his own life and about his own ideals.[32] While most critics attack 'Proshchanie s Materoi' from an artistic point of view, E. Sidorov states bluntly that Rasputin's 'tendentiousness has overstepped the limitations of objectivity.'[33]

Rasputin disagrees, of course, with many of these accusations. While he concedes that there is no return to Matera because it has been flooded anyway, he claims that he is not preoccupied with the defence of the old village, as many critics presume, but rather with 'the spiritual world of millions which is being transformed and is disappearing altogether, and which tomorrow will be different from what it is today.'[34] Rasputin considers it the writer's duty to immortalize this difficult process, and to leave its account to posterity. He refutes his critics by saying that 'an artist could only be an artist because he sees objects not the way he wants to see them, but the way they really are.'[35]

Until the appearance of 'Proshchanie s Materoi' Rasputin's place in current Soviet literature was secure and safe. His artistic gift was recognized, and his creative independence respected. He enjoyed the patronage of a number of leading Moscow writers, including past residents of Siberia, such as Sergei Zalygin and others;[36] and he was rapidly reaching for the summit of Soviet letters. 'Proshchanie s Materoi' and the severe ideological criticism it has encountered are an indication that while Rasputin's position remains unique, his further artistic growth will depend largely on his ability to adapt his talent to the requirements of official criticism and editorial control. It is not easy for any writer to relinquish his artistic freedom, the more so if one creates in the manner in which Rasputin does. He never prepares in advance any plan or scheme for a work of art. He never knows how his plot will develop, just as he does not know what the next day will bring.[37] Thus his creative process appears to be impulsive, sometimes even subconscious and unpredictable, and the resulting work of art does not lend itself easily to outside regulation or prescription.

6 ❖ Iurii Trifonov: City prose

Iurii Trifonov is one of the most widely read, most discussed, and perhaps most controversial of Soviet writers. He was born in 1925, lost his parents in the purges of the 1930s, worked during the war in an aircraft factory, and studied after the war at the Gorky Literary Institute in Moscow. His first published works were written as early as 1947, and his first major appearance on the Soviet literary scene dates back to 1950, when his novel *Studenty* (Students) (1950)[1] was published in *Novyi mir*.

Studenty, a novel in which the student life at a Moscow institute in the immediate post-war period is depicted, was an exemplary product of socialist realism, as was recognized by Soviet officialdom in awarding the book the Stalin Prize for literature. Trifonov's second major work, *Utolenie zhazhdy* (The Quenching of Thirst) (1963),[2] deals with the construction of the Kara Kum Canal in Central Asia. The title of the novel has a double meaning. It refers to the thirst for water by the desert as well as to a thirst for truth and justice which have been missing in this land for many years.

The latest period in the evolution of Trifonov's art, the period of his maturity, begins in 1966 with the appearance of the stories 'Vera i Zoika' (Vera and Zoika) and 'Byl letnii polden'' (A Summer Mid-day)[3] published in *Novyi mir*, then still under the editorship of Aleksandr Tvardovskii. These stories were followed by 'V gribnuiu osen'' (In the Mushroom Picking Season) (1968),[4] 'Obmen' (1969),[5] 'Predvaritel'nye itogi' (1970),[6] 'Dolgoe proshchnie' (1971),[7] 'Drugaia zhizn'' (Another Life) (1975),[8] 'Dom na naberezhnoi' (The House on the Embankment) (1976),[9] and *Starik* (The Old Man) (1978).[10] The return of Trifonov, after more than a decade, to *Novyi mir* and his renewed association with Aleksandr Tvardovskii[11] have had a positive effect on the growth of his artistic talent and have fostered a new development in his art.

The short stories 'Vera i Zoika,' 'Byl letnii polden',' and 'V gribnuiu osen'' are, in a way, an introduction to the major *povesti* which begin with 'Obmen.' These stories lack the deep psychological analysis charactersitic of Trifonov's recent prose. They give instead a brief impressionistic account of certain events, leaving the reader to contemplate the fate of the heroes. The plots of these stories are simple and uncomplicated. Few characters participate in the action and we know little about their past.

Yet despite the sketchy treatment of his heroes, Trifonov succeeds in creating a certain mood, an atmosphere which renders well the complexity of human nature as well as the inability of one man to understand his fellow men. We learn from these stories that each man has his own problems, each tries to cope with life in a different manner. People endowed with an innate nobility of character, regardless of their station in life, usually minimize the importance of their own difficulties and seek to help others; by contrast, most people relate to others in a manner which reflects only their personal interests. Each person reacts differently to his or her own circumstances.

'Vera i Zoika' is an episode in the life of several women representing different social groups. Despite external differences, there is much in common in their fates; each woman, however, reacts to life in a different manner. In 'Byl letnii polden',' an encounter of two old women, good friends who have not seen each other for fifty years, is depicted. The women renew their acquaintance by going back to the day when they parted. Much has happened during the fifty years, much has changed, and yet, after a while, there is a feeling that they have never parted at all. Such changes as have occurred are predominantly external.

In 'V gribnuiu osen'' the death of the mother makes one realize that the daughter misses her mother mostly because there is no one to perform the many tasks around the house which have been for many years the mother's responsibility. The mother-daughter relationship has been built not on genuine love and affection, but on the principle of need and usefulness. When the mother was alive she was taken for granted, and only after her death has the daughter come to realize that her mother is irreplaceable. There is no blunt message in these stories, just a simple episodic portrayal of daily life. Under the surface, however, there is a hint at man's imperfection; also an intimation that while on the surface all men are similar, in essence no two creatures are the same.

Most of Trifonov's works of the last decade have much in common with his earlier writings, but they contain a number of new artistic elements. His main heroes are usually city-dwellers, most of them well-educated professional people. The emphasis is on the personal lives of the heroes, while their work and their social and professional concerns are left in the background. Family problems, infidelity, narrow-minded egotism, and the sacrifice of spiritual values for material well-being are a rule rather than an exception in these works. The actions of the protagonists outside the narrow circle of their families often express the same negative qualities which are visible in the situations of family life.

In addition, in many recent works Trifonov expresses an interest in history. A number of his heroes study Russia's revolutionary past, and the writer contrasts in his works the high moral values professed by the revolutionaries with the ethical shallowness of Soviet man today. Several works and, in particular, 'Otblesk kostra' (Reflection of a Bonfire) (1965)[12] and the novel *Neterpenie* (1973),[13] are specifically devoted to Russia's past and are somewhat outside the mainstream of Trifonov's most recent concerns.

The Trifonov of the last decade is vastly different from the man who created *Studenty* and even *Utolenie zhazhdy*. The new Trifonov endeavours to present a truthful and realistic picture of Soviet life without minimizing the complexity of the human relationships facing Soviet man. Trifonov has practically abandoned the old precepts of socialist realism by refusing to suggest positive solutions and by declining to make a clear choice. He continues in his new works to concern himself with ethical problems, but no longer juxtaposes his negative characters with positive ones, a contrasting device often used to elevate the positive hero and to make him appear in a better light than he really deserves. The new Trifonov treats all his characters with understanding and compassion. It is the approach of a writer who has learned to appreciate his own imperfection and the limitations and shortcomings of his fellow beings.

Most of his recent plots are simple, and deal with common problems and situations deeply rooted in Soviet life. The uninitiated Western reader may have difficulty in deciphering the meaning of these narratives. In 'Obmen' the main conflict centres around an intended exchange of living quarters, which are in great demand in Moscow. Dmitriev, his wife Lena, and their young daughter occupy a single room. Similarly Dmitriev's mother, Ksenia Fedorovna, has one room. Lena and her mother-in-law are not on speaking terms and yet, realizing that Ksenia Fedorovna has cancer and that her days are numbered, Lena urges Dmitriev to convince his mother to exchange their separate rooms for a two-room apartment. After their mother's death, the Dmitrievs could then retain the apartment instead of the single room they presently occupy. The exchange is by no means a simple operation. It involves a number of illegal machinations and requires the assistance of an outside 'operator.' Dmitriev knows that what he is doing is unethical and unlawful but all the same he goes ahead with the plan. Ksenia Fedorovna dies soon after the exchange has been consummated but Dmitriev himself comes down with an illness and is confined for several weeks to a hospital bed.

Dmitriev is pretending to be honest, but under the pressure of Lena he acts in the manner most expedient at any given moment. There is nothing sacred to him if only in the long run things work out to his advantage. On one occasion, when Dmitriev visits his mother and tries to impress upon her the mutual advantages of the exchange, Ksenia Fedorovna retorts: 'You already made an exchange, Vitia. The exchange has occurred ... It was a long time ago.'[14] She obviously alludes to the change which has taken place in the character and behaviour of her son, who little by little gives up the spiritual values and the lofty ideals of his own family for the 'pragmatism' of his wife and her parents.

Trifonov has introduced a new term to describe such a process: *olukianit'sia*, taken from the surname of Lena's parents. The Lukianovs represent a special breed of Soviet city-dwellers. They are people who 'know how to live,' who have the necessary connections and manage to arrange their lives in a most comfortable way. Such people often walk on the brink of the law, though they are careful not to overstep it; but they completely ignore the unwritten moral laws on which community life is based. The Lukianovs are no longer young. They were born and grew up in tsarist Russia and they could be regarded as remnants of the past. It is often said that their behaviour and actions are influenced by their bourgeois consciousness. Most characters in Trifonov's other recent works, however, regardless of their age, station in life, or social background, are also people who consider it a virtue 'to know how to live' and who adhere to a code of so-called ethics designed to satisfy their personal needs.

The Soviet critic, Feliks Kuznetsov, views 'Obmen' as a success. He suggests that 'the importance of this story lies in its confirmation of a new, genuinely humane morality.'[15] He claims that 'due to his inner weakness and lack of principles, Dmitriev gives in to the pressures of his wife Lena who is the very embodiment of the lack of spirituality.'[16] By ascribing Dmitriev's behaviour and actions only to his ethical shallowness and to Lena's lack of spirituality, Kuznetsov is not being strictly consistent with the requirements of Soviet literary theory, according to which social conditions are a moving force of social phenomena as well as of man's actions. 'Obmen' is highly regarded in the Soviet Union because the actions of Dmitriev and Lena can be considered as the shortcomings of individuals and are by no means characteristic of society in general. Such an interpretation is possible because in the background of the plot there is the outstanding family of Dmitriev's mother as well as Dmitriev's grandfather, who embodies all the lofty ideals of a dedicated revolutionary.

Since 1969, however, nothing of this kind is encountered in Trifonov's works depicting Soviet reality. The main subject of 'Predvaritel'nye itogi' is the morality of those representing the Soviet world of letters and higher education. In 'Dolgoe proshchanie,' we become acquainted with the unwritten laws of Moscow theatre life. Most of these conventions are base, unethical, and unjust; they work in favour of unscrupulous people, who have mastered the art of 'how to live,' but against those who have not yet learned to compromise with their conscience.

Against the nasty social background of these plots, the personal dramas of the heroes are depicted. In 'Predvaritel'nye itogi' we are exposed to a family in which there is no mutual love, respect, or understanding. The main protagonist Gennadii

Sergeevich, a translator of poetry, his well-educated wife Rita, and their student son are strangers to each other. The only thing they have in common is a self-centred egotism and a lack of basic moral values. Each lives his own life with little regard for others. There is no wonder that such atmosphere leads to constant quarrels and breeds family instability.

The title 'Predvaritel'nye itogi' is apposite. At the end of the story a reconciliation between husband and wife takes place. It appears that the translator, who has already been married and divorced once before and who suffers from a heart ailment, does not want to be bothered with another divorce; it is too much for him. He prefers temporary peace to further complications. The composition of the family and its spiritual shallowness, however, are such that one feels the reprieve is only temporary; that the happy ending of the story is but a calm before the next storm and that, accordingly, it is too early to draw a final line in the history of this family.

The main protagonist of 'Dolgoe proshchanie' is the good-natured actress Lialia Telepneva. For a number of years she has lived as the common-law wife of an unsuccessful script-writer, Grisha Rebrov. Lialia's mother is against their marriage. She taunts Rebrov continuously for his inability to support her daughter and forces the latter to have a number of abortions. In the end Rebrov realizes that Lialia is unfaithful to him. He is unwilling to share her favours with those who help her career, and he leaves her to go to Siberia.

Many years later Rebrov becomes a famous playwright while Lialia, having abandoned her career, is married to a military man. Neither of them, however, is happy; life appeared to be better when they were young and together. The fate of Lialia and Grisha indicates clearly the elusiveness of happiness. The interference of Lialia's mother, the pressures of immoral social conventions which demanded Lialia's submission, and Lialia's nature, ready to satisfy everyone who needed her favours, force the breakup of a relationship between two people who, though they had faults, did at least appear to care for each other.

Trifonov's recent works – 'Drugaia zhizn'' and 'Dom na naberezhnoi' – are artistically his most mature works. In the writer's own words, he 'succeeded in expressing in them, as clearly as possible, the general phenomenon of life.'[17] A discussion of these works makes it possible to draw certain conclusions about the place of Trifonov in the Soviet literature of today and about the most recent development of his art.

The picture of the main hero of 'Drugaia zhizn',' Sergei Troitskii, is given through the eyes of his wife Olga. Sergei is an able and honest man who would never sacrifice his conscience for the tangible advantages of this world, but he is also a strange man who has difficulty in finding a place for himself in life. Sergei's life is further complicated by his relationship with his wife, who loves him deeply but is also terribly jealous. Olga suspects every woman in sight of a relationship with her husband, trying, at the same time, to convince herself that she trusts him. Her suspicions and doubts, which are usually groundless, are irrational.

She follows Sergei everywhere to keep a constant check on him. She thinks she does this for his sake, for the sake of their love, but she is driven to it by her irrational fear of another woman in her husband's life. One of Sergei's ostensible girl friends tells Olga: 'If you drive your husband to death, that is your business. But I will destroy you if you do not leave me and my husband in peace.'[18] These words are prophetic. Sergei is driven to his death at the age of forty-two. His 'friends' at work, his wife's 'love,' and his inability to find a place for himself in life are the causes of his death. Before his death, when he is forced to resign his job at the institute because of his involvement in spiritualism, Sergei says that it is all for the better; that it is necessary to begin 'a new life [druguiu zhizn'] for which there already remains little time.'[19] There is no need to worry. Sergei's tranquility is now unperturbed; his 'new life' is eternal.

The title of the story is symbolic and perhaps pessimistic, implying that it is difficult, if not impossible, to change man's nature. There is no reasonable explanation why one human being has the inner capacity for happiness while another does not. It appears that the author does not believe in the possibility of a real change in the protagonists or in a new relationship between them. He concludes, therefore, that a true renewal is possible for Sergei only after his death.

The most important element in 'Drugaia zhizn'' is Trifonov's ability to render convincingly the complexity of human relationships. Being a master of psychological analysis, he demonstrates clearly that excellent intentions are not enough to build a good relationship; that the irrational elements in human nature are often stronger than most reasonable convictions and decisions. He writes that 'every marriage – is not a union of two people, as is presumed, but rather a union or collision of two clans, of two worlds.'[20] This union or collision becomes even more complicated because man strives all his life to understand his fellow man without realizing that he is unable even to understand himself.

In the background of the human drama, the work of a scientific research institute is described. Sergei's friend Klimuk, the graduate secretary of the institute, suggests that Sergei give up part of his research material, gathered for his kandidat dissertation, to the associate director of the institute, Kislovskii. Klimuk makes it plain that it is better to surrender some of the material required for Kislovskii's doctoral dissertation than to forfeit the chance of defending his own thesis. Sergei is furious; he cannot compromise with his conscience. Not so Klimuk, who later uses the evidence about the intended transfer of material in order to unseat Kislovskii from his job and to get himself promoted to the position of associate director.

Trifonov's next novelette, 'Dom na naberezhnoi,' is in many respects similar to the other works discussed here. Trifonov deals here with the same human material, similar problems, and the same time span as in *Studenty*. His approach to the events and his treatment of the heroes here, however, are completely different. The evolution of Trifonov, man and writer, is most visible when comparing these two works. At the centre of 'Dom na naberezhnoi' is the problem of the ethics of today's Soviet urban population, a problem at the root of all Trifonov's works since 'Obmen.' In 'Dom na naberezhnoi' the author investigates the development of a literary bureaucrat. He follows the actions of his hero and the forces which influence his development from early childhood to maturity. Trifonov analyses the creation of a literary scholar who is without convictions or moral principles, a man of many different faces.

The hero of 'Dom na naberezhnoi,' Vadim Glebov, grows up on a small street in Moscow. At school Glebov makes friends among the hoodlums as well as among the well-behaved children who live in a nearby apartment house. After the war Glebov enrols in an institute to study literature. He learns that Professor Ganchuk, who lives in the apartment house and whose daughter Sonia has been his classmate, is now head of a department in the same institute. In childhood Sonia had been deeply in love with Glebov, but he hardly paid any attention to her. Now a friendship with Sonia could help his professional advancement. Glebov begins to frequent the home of the Ganchuks where he becomes obsessed with the idea that all the material possessions accumulated by Sonia's parents could be his. He starts a love affair with Sonia without actually loving her. She is now included in his scheme of becoming the sole heir to the Ganchuks' wealth.

Glebov's calculations lead nowhere. At that very time the administration of the institute, represented by its most unworthy people, starts a campaign against the so-called 'cosmopolitans' in literature. Several good scholars and teachers are expelled. Ganchuk takes up their defence but he does not have to wait long for retribution. He is severely attacked by the bureaucrats and is removed from his position, while Glebov is called upon to spy on his future father-in-law and to denounce him in public.

The relationship of Glebov and Sonia of course breaks up. There is no place for her any more in Glebov's calculations. She becomes ill and soon dies; so does her old mother who has been teaching German in the institute. At the end of the narrative, many years later, in 1974, we encounter Glebov on his way to Paris to participate in an international congress of literary scholars, while the eighty-six-year-old Ganchuk visits the grave of his daughter and wonders about the absurdity of his existence. Sonia is dead while he is still alive and wants to go on living.

The parallels and distinctions between *Studenty* and 'Dom na naberezhnoi' are evident. There are many similar problems discussed in these two works but the solutions are completely different. In *Studenty* Professor Kozelskii is accused by his colleagues and students alike of formalism, aestheticism, and cosmopolitanism. The best people in the institute are against him. The main positive hero, Belov, is instrumental in helping to force Kozelskii out of the institute. The nature of the novel is such that Kozelskii appears to be in the wrong in that he hates Soviet literature and Soviet students. He is almost an enemy of the people. In 'Dom na naberezhnoi' Professor Astrug is accused of similar transgressions but the best people in the institute stand up in his defence. They are unsuccessful in their endeavour and some are even penalized for this attempt; but they are bold enough to say what they think. In *Studenty* Kozelskii appears to be in the wrong, while in 'Dom na naberezhnoi' the conspiracy of the administration against Professor Ganchuk and his friends is portrayed as groundless.

Artistically, Trifonov's latest works are vastly superior to works such as *Studenty*. In *Studenty* the characterization was inadequate, the conflicts were resolved in an unconvincing manner, and journalistic clichés formed the major part of the narrative. In his latest works Trifonov creates real people with real problems. He presents the human relationships of his heroes in all their complexity and he creates in each work a special atmosphere which is characteristic of the given situation. It is often suggested that Trifonov's heroes are transparent, that we see through them, that the writer uses the X-ray technique to reveal their souls and minds. This view has been encouraged by Trifonov's transition from third-person to first-person narration. Trifonov claims that personal narration permits him to penetrate deeper into the souls of his characters.

The similarity between Trifonov's recent works is not limited to their range of themes. Most of them also have a similar structure. They usually begin with a short introduction in which the narrator tells something about the present position of the characters, after which he proceeds to reveal their past in the form of reminiscences or straightforward third-person narrative. On the last few pages the author brings us back to the beginning of the story.

'Obmen' begins and ends with the illness of Dmitriev's mother, and it covers approximately one year. In between there is a temporary improvement in her health, just long enough to consummate the exchange and to tell the history of the protagonists. Most of the story is told in the third person, with the narrator appearing in the conclusion to tell in the first person about his recent meeting with Dmitriev and of the latter's illness following the exchange. 'Predvaritel'nye itogi' is narrated in the first person in the form of reminiscences. It begins with the description of the translator's present-day situation, followed by a flashback in which we are told his life story. In the conclusion we return to the initial circumstances which are related in a manner which makes it difficult to distinguish between reality and dream. In 'Dolgoe proshchanie,' which is narrated in the third person, the introduction and conclusion take place in the late sixties, while most of the action relates to the heroes' experiences in the early fifties.

The structural pattern: present – past – present, is also employed by Trifonov in his next two stories. 'in 'Drugaia zhizn' ' we are introduced at the beginning to Sergei's wife who grieves over her husband's death. Then, in the form of a flashback, we are given an account of their relationship and the events leading to Sergei's death. In conclusion we are again with Olga who is in a state of vacillation between reality and dream.

In 'Dom na naberezhnoi' the basic structural pattern is similar but it is more complex and intricate. The story begins in 1972 and ends in 1974, but the action covers some forty years, in particular the thirties and forties. The story is narrated on several different levels, and there is a constant transition from the present to the past and back, with a multitude of digressions and changes in the sequence of time and narration. The narrator is a minor character. He resides in the house on the embankment, appearing only from time to time to qualify the events and actions of the protagonists or to tell something about himself.

There is in 'Dom na naberezhnoi' a fine line between reality and fiction, the author using the narrator to relate elements of his own past which have remained vivid in his memory from early childhood. In particular, this is true of the story concerning the narrator's expulsion from his apartment to a single room in a remote district. Trifonov's father, a participant in the civil war, was indeed purged in the late thirties and his mother arrested. The young Trifonov remained behind with his grandmother, but they had to leave the apartment house which was reserved for important dignitaries.

At the centre of all Trifonov's recent plots there is usually a couple: a man and a woman who live together but who find themselves in a complex relationship which is doomed to failure. In 'Obmen' there is another woman in the life of Dmitriev, and his marriage with Lena is held together only by their common offspring and common living quarters. There is no true affection in their marriage, only a realization of the advantage of living together. In 'Predvaritel'nye itogi' the marriage between Gennadii Sergeevich and Rita is in a precarious state and one can suspect that it will not survive too long. In 'Dolgoe proshchanie' Rebrov leaves Lialia, and in 'Dom na naberezhnoi' Glebov forsakes Sonia, while in 'Drugaia zhizn' ' Olga is widowed by the sudden death of her husband.

In most cases the women are stronger and more possessive than their mates, and they lead their partners to downfall. Thus Lena is, in a way, the cause of Dmitriev's moral downfall, while Rita is to a large extent the cause of the translator's ill-health and his disillusionment with life. Lialia and Sonia are different; they are submissive and compassionate, ever ready to help their fellow humans, but unable to distinguish between a real friend and an enemy.

There are no strong positive men among the leading protagonists. Most of them drift along in life and submit to the pressures of existence. Dmitriev and the translator submit to the immoral designs of their spouses, while Sergei is crushed by the circumstances of life. Rebrov escapes this fate, not because he is a strong character, but because he runs away from reality. Instead of facing the challenge and putting up a fight for the woman he loves, he abandons her to fate. Glebov, also, is not a man of character; he is a shrewd opportunist with a strong sense of self-preservation. This behaviour suggests that, regardless of personal traits, there is an inherent instability in most families. As one character suggests: 'The contemporary marriage is a most tender institution. The idea of an easy parting and an attempt to start everything from the beginning, before it is too late, is constantly in the air.'[21]

Trifonov writes about the Soviet urban intelligentsia and uses the language of this social group. He writes in a simple and direct manner, making good use of dialogue. His prose is infused with irony. He relies little on folklore, symbolism, or figures of speech. Instead there is in his language an emphasis on the new idiom of Soviet man: an idiom created by the conditions of life and a new social awareness, a language coined for the expression of peculiar phenomena characteristic of the Soviet way of life. The development of Trifonov the artist is little affected by the evolution of his language, which has in essence changed very little. His prose continues to remain simple but his characters become more complex and the structure of his plots more intricate.

The emphasis in Trifonov's recent prose is on the everyday life of the protagonists, but many of his heroes have outside interests not related to their personal lives. For some, such as Rita, these interests are an escape from boredom. Her obsession with old icons and monasteries is not inspired by a real interest in Russia's past, but rather by her desire to be in tune with the times, to do what is fashionable. Many other characters, however, have a genuine interest in Russian history and, in particular, in its revolutionary past. Thus Sergei's dissertation deals with the history of Russia in the immediate pre-revolutionary period. Grisha Rebrov is an eager student of the populist movement in Russia; he studies with care the lives and deeds of Pryzhov and Kletochnikov. Rebrov is so absorbed with the study of the past that he hardly notices what happens today. The elements of history in Trifonov's prose are often overlooked in the analysis of his work, but the preoccupation of his characters with the past is an expression of the author's own deep concern and interest in the history of his country.

The appearance of Trifonov's historical novel, *Neterpenie*, was a complete surprise to many readers. Yet it is not difficult to detect the connection between this novel and Trifonov's city prose. Some characters in *Neterpenie* – in particular, Nikolai Vasil'evich Kletochnikov, who infiltrates the tsarist secret police to assist the revolutionary cause – have been mentioned in Trifonov's earlier works. The main hero is Andrei Zheliabov, the leader of a group which organized the assassination of the tsar.

The novel is rooted in historical reality with very little resort to fiction. It is told in the third person with a number of lyrical digressions narrated in the first person, in which the author updates us on the further fate of his heroes and gives us a current view of past events. The novel is written in the language Trifonov uses for his urban prose. The author sees in this method an expression of the unity of times. He claims that 'there is an inner connection between the novel *Neterpenie* and the city stories ... The connection between these divergent themes is to be found in the ethical sphere.'[22] According to Trifonov the past and the future are fused together in today's reality. Our present existence is influenced by the past as well as by our concern for the future.

Trifonov's latest short novel, *Starik*, gives further evidence of the writer's concern with the investigation and artistic fusion of the Soviet *byt* with the historical past of the Russian people. The action in *Starik* takes place in two different periods, fifty-five years apart. The main protagonist of the novel is the pensioner Pavel Evgrafovich Letunov, a veteran of the civil war. His life is uneventful. He is surrounded by his children, their friends and neighbours, all of whom are engulfed in an intricate web of the *byt*; everyone trying to deal with the complexities of life in a manner which exhibits a total lack of scruples or moral principles and which usually brings out the worst Philistine traits in those concerned.

Everyday life brings little happiness or contentment and the old man seeks an escape in his reminiscences about the past. He tries to unearth all the available information on the fate of the cossack revolutionary leader Migulin, unjustly condemned to death by a revolutionary court and subsequently shot during the civil war. Pavel Evgrafovich is driven in his pursuit by a sense of guilt and by his conscience, because he was one of those who participated in the trial of Migulin and who believed in the cossack leader's guilt. Now, after having himself been unjustly purged in the days of Stalin, Letunov begins to realize that Migulin has been a victim of circumstances, and he tries to do everything in his power to have the cossack revolutionary rehabilitated.

Starik has a number of artistic shortcomings. The integration of the past with the present is far from perfect. There are different groups of heroes in the two periods discussed – with the old people, Letunov and his friend and Migulin's wife Asia, only sketchily drawn.

Yet the novel has a number of positive artistic elements and it forms a new step in

Trifonov's investigation of the revolutionary past of the Soviet state. The loosely connected structure of the narrative, the constant transition from the present to the past, and the continuous shift from third-person to first-person narration express well the instability of the time, the insecurity of man, and the unpredictability of fate.

Pavel Evgrafovich is baffled by the helplessness of man, by his inability to make a rational distinction between what seems to be the truth and what appears to be a lie. He is frustrated by the fact that most things in life and in history are judged in extreme terms: everything is black or white with nothing in between, while in reality there are elements of both, goodness and evil, the positive and the negative, in everything and in everyone. The reminiscences of Letunov and his analysis of past events could lead the reader to conclusions which are very much in the spirit of Leo Tolstoi's interpretation of history. Man is a blind tool of circumstances. He participates in historical events, deluding himself that he is in possession of the truth, while in reality he is only emotionally attached to a cause without being able to make a rational decision about the real course of events.

Trifonov claims that his art is in the tradition of nineteenth-century classical literature. He feels that he is also indebted to the writers of the 1920s and 1930s, and in particular to Andrei Platonov, Isaak Babel', and Aleksei Tolstoi. He sees his place in today's Soviet literature as that of one who follows in the tradition of Anton Chekhov and the writers of the 1920s. He asserts that he struggles for a very high level of expressiveness in his works. He strives to say much in very few words and he claims that a short work may often contain more meaning than a large novel. Trifonov suggests that 'Chekhov's best stories are nothing but novels pressed together by the tremendous force of his art. While, at the same time, there are many long novels which are in essence stretched-out stories in which the action evolves around a single event, covering just a few days. Thus it appears that the novel and the story have equal potential for depicting life.'[23] Indeed, Chekhov's influence is evident in Trifonov's latest works. The lack of a direct social message, the atmosphere of mutual misunderstanding and inability to communicate, the predilection for understatement – so characteristic of Chekhov's stories – are all part of Trifonov's recent work.

The development of Trifonov the artist has been a slow process. Early in his literary career he thought that to produce a good work of art it was essential to find a good plot. Later he decided that appropriate words are just as important as a good plot. The mature Trifonov has come to the conclusion that 'the main difficulty in writing prose is in finding ideas ... One must have something to say; to communicate something important to the reader.'[24] According to him, the most important aspect of writing is not how to build a phrase or find an appropriate conclusion, but the ability to build a life and to create a fate as truthful to life as possible.[25]

Trifonov claims that in his early works there was a certain interrelationship and coherency. 'One thing was connected with another; one thing would emanate from another. But in this coherency there was also a *constraint* ... Now I aim at depth, at remote connections, which the reader should discover and guess by himself.'[26] Trifonov's new approach to his art makes possible the publication of his controversial works in the Soviet Union, but it also leaves him open to the attacks of official critics. Most of his recent works have been accepted for publication, because there is often less said in them than is alluded to, because more is left beneath the surface (*podtekst*) than is written.

Trifonov's works usually generate a strong and mixed reaction in the Soviet Union. Most critics demand from him a clear artistic statement as to where he stands in relation to his characters. One critic claimed that 'the separation of the personal from the social [in 'Drugaia zhizn' '] makes it impossible to depict the social conditions of psychological upheavals; therefore, the reader is deprived of the possibility to decide for himself the real reasons for human misunderstanding and inability to communicate.'[27] Another critic attacked Trifonov for separating *byt*, or everyday life, from other social and ideological problems in 'Dom na naberezhnoi.'

N. Klado wrote in *Literaturnaia gazeta* that he has no argument with Trifonov's characters but rather with the author himself for showing his protagonists in an incomplete light. He asserted that 'the separation of the heroes from their ideological interests and social connections and, most of all, from their work [*dela*] is, just as any *incompleteness*, similar to the amputation of a part of a living body which leads to a situation in which the whole body loses, while the detached part cannot go on existing independently.'[28] Klado probably wanted Trifonov to provide a positive hero with a definite statement in favour of the present policies of the Communist Party and the Soviet government. He failed to realize that Trifonov mainly concerns himself with human problems and not with social schemes and events. In addition, any positive statement or lofty ideals pronounced by people such as Glebov would surely sound like sheer hypocrisy.

'Dom na naberezhnoi' has been singled out for strong criticism because it is possible to infer from it that the Soviet system facilitates the actions and behaviour of those who forsake their own beliefs and ethical principles in order to support a given course of action by the party and government. The conclusion of the story is an obvious reminder that although much that was wrong had taken place in the days of Stalin, those most guilty of it avoided retribution. Thus Sonia and her mother are dead, old Ganchuk is a broken man; while Glebov, a distinguished scholar but a man without a conscience or ethical principles, lectures others on the importance of ethics and morality, continuing at the same time to live in his old ways. It is no wonder that the character of Glebov irritates certain representatives of the Soviet literary establishment. Many of those who in the past ardently supported Stalin and his literary policies probably recognize themselves in the image of this 'literary scholar.'

'Dom na naberezhnoi' is one of the few works criticized at the Sixth Congress of Soviet Writers in June 1976. Thus, for example, in his report to the congress, G.M. Markov praised Trifonov's 'Obmen' and placed it next to Aitmatov's 'Belyi parokhod'; but he also said that the plot and form of 'Dom na naberezhnoi' were conceived in such a manner that 'the heroes as well as the readers are deprived of the possibility of becoming fully aware that there exists another force which is able to help alleviate what might seem like hopeless fates and desperate situations. In this case it is not a question of form or genre but of the writer's philosophical views.'[29] Similarly, V. Ozerov accused Trifonov of creating 'people who act in a kind of spiritual vacuum; people who are hermetically locked up in their own environment, while the author remains purposely on the sidelines, covering up his own intentions.'[30]

Thus Trifonov is attacked for failing to show that in the background there is a positive force which has the necessary answers to all questions and the means required to solve all problems. In 'Dom na naberezhnoi' there is no positive background, and no positive heroes. There are in fact few positive heroes in Soviet literature who are truly believable and realistic. It is difficult to create the image of a positive man. Dostoevskii struggled with this problem all his life and the results of his efforts are well-known. Similarly, Trifonov refuses to categorize his protagonists; he says that it is possible to classify literary characters but not human beings.[31] Everybody is different. He thus attempts to describe in his latest works real human beings as they are rather than as they should be.

The term *byt* is often contrasted in Russian and Soviet literary criticism with the term *bytie*. While *bytie* refers to the life or existence of a human being in general, including all his social, economic, ideological, personal, and other concerns, the term *byt* refers only to certain aspects of one's personal existence. Official Soviet criticism has come out strongly against the proliferation of *byt* literature in the last decade.[32] Trifonov himself resents the inclusion of his works in *byt* literature. He claims that the division of Soviet literature into different trends (*napravleniia*) is artificial. The recent application of the term *byt* in literature, he feels, has been devised by Soviet theorists of literature who are often far removed from the realities of literary practice.

Trifonov asserts that 'if *byt* is life, even everyday life, then I write about my own life or about the lives of my acquaintances, about people I know well. In addition, there is no clear explanation of what is now understood by the term *byt*. If *byt* refers, for example, only to cooking dinner for the family or going to the store to do some shopping then it is one thing, but if *byt* refers also to one's family and personal life, to love and happiness or illness and death, then *Anna Karenina* could also be considered as the depiction of *byt*.' Trifonov is right in comparing the personal dramas of his heroes with those of nineteenth-century literature. He does not mention, however, that in *Anna Karenina* the search for the meaning of life, the quest for God, the discussion of problems of life, happiness, and death are all a part of *byt*, a part of everyday life.

No discussion of such problems is possible in Soviet literature because the answers to such problems are predetermined. It is claimed that the development of Soviet society is economically conditioned and, as Klimuk suggests, man's actions should be determined by historical expediency. To which Sergei retorts: 'It is interesting to know who is going to decide what is expedient and what is not. Perhaps the Learned Council [of the Institute] by a majority vote.'[33] That is probably as far as one can go in discussing problems of social theory and ideology in Soviet literature.

It is interesting to note that Trifonov resents the fact that most Western critics overemphasize the social aspects of his work at the expense of the literary qualities of his art. It is paradoxical that most Soviet critics use a similar approach in their discussion of his work. The reasons for this similar approach are completely different. Western critics view Trifonov's prose as a reflection of Soviet reality in the 1970s. One should not be surprised at the interest of Western readers in such literature. It is almost the only source from which to reconstruct a picture of the life, values, and concerns of the Soviet city-dweller. Several decades ago there was no such possibility because the social message, a positive hero, and a varnished reality were the heart of any Soviet work of art. Thus the lack of a definite social message in Trifonov's works gives the Western reader the possibility to decide for himself the real problems and preoccupations of Soviet man.

To most Soviet critics, however, the lack of a positive message is a shortcoming which could lead the uninitiated reader to wrong conclusions. Not all Soviet critics, however, censure Trifonov for his alleged shortcomings. Some have words of high praise, seeing in him one of the best Soviet writers today, while others criticize him but do not fail to give due credit to his artistic mastery. Thus, for example, A. Bocharov disagrees with those who attack Trifonov for his emphasis on *byt*. He claims that Trifonov is not concerned only with the depiction of everyday life; instead, 'his main attention is attracted to the *emotional experiences* of man in situations of everyday life. These emotional experiences form the true inner force moving the plots of his works.'[34] M. Sinel'nikov, however, writes in *Voprosy literatury* that 'Iu. Trifonov is very precise in fulfilling his artistic objectives, in depicting the inner world of his heroes, in analysing the most secret and cherished movements of their souls. However, he is not always exact, and he often even contradicts himself when dealing with aspects of human relationships and with conflicts which require a deep insight and understanding of social phenomena.'[35]

It is possible to conclude that Trifonov the writer develops in step with the development of Trifonov the man. The Chekhovian approach to the treatment of human problems developed in him slowly and it became prominent only in the last decade. Indeed, in the 'Author's Preface' to the English translation of *Studenty*, Trifonov notes that Sergei Palavin is 'a "negative" type whose attitudes are a harmful hang-over from an earlier period ... We are bound to remark them in order to remake them and take them with us into the bright future when communism will have been achieved.'[36] A quarter of a century later Trifonov has given up the idea of changing the 'negative' hero. He does not divide his heroes any more into 'positive' and 'negative.' He alludes to the fact that no one is perfect and that many people have negative qualities which it is necessary to counteract. He refuses even to acknowledge that Lena, the main culprit of 'Obmen,' is a negative character; he says that she has good as well as bad traits of character, a fact which makes her even more human.[37]

The struggle between positive and negative characters in Trifonov's early works turns now into a struggle between the good and the bad qualities in man, into a struggle between goodness and evil. Trifonov is explicit in stating that it is possible to change a social order and the economic conditions of a people, but it is much more difficult to change the very essence of man. He says: 'let us not delude ourselves; in order to heal a disease such as egotism in man we will need many, many years. Egotism is surely the oldest disease inflicted upon the human race.'[38] He quotes Michail Lermontov, who said that he presents problems but is far from suggesting a remedy for them.[39] Trifonov remarks that he also presents problems, mainly ethical problems, in the hope that they will teach people something and will prompt them to think at least for a moment about their own shortcomings and behaviour. This is, according to him, the first step toward a moral regeneration of man.

The evolution of Trifonov's artistic method and his new approach to the treatment of his heroes are the result of the changes which have taken place in the Soviet Union in the post-Stalin period. In *Studenty* the message was explicit because no other literature was possible at that time. In *Utolenie zhazhdy* Trifonov again was in tune with the times as he paid tribute to the spirit of the Twentieth Party Congress, and to the leadership of Khrushchev. Now, more than two decades later, he realizes that the post-Stalin reforms have changed the Soviet system and the essence of Soviet man very little and that one of the main shortcomings of Soviet society is the shallowness of the ethical values professed by most Soviet citizens. He has turned to a kind of literature in which there are few positive heroes, but in which there is a hidden call for self-perfection. This is a call for Soviet man to preserve his human face and his dignity. Trifonov's art evolved in the mainstream of Soviet literature. Until the late sixties his writing very much reflected the situation existing in Soviet society in general, and in Soviet literature in particular. Trifonov's works of the last decade, however, are an expression of the growing disparity between literary theory and practice as well as of the search for a new image of man.[40]

A number of Trifonov's characters spend their lives in a continuous search for happiness, for the meaning of life. But few actually attain the desired state of contentment and tranquillity. People such as Sergei from 'Drugaia zhizn' ' are subdued by daily life and by social pressures. They are unable to overcome the inherent contradictions between their individualistic natures and social convention. Others, like Dmitriev or Glebov, sacrifice spiritual for immediate material benefits, but it is doubtful whether the material well-being they achieve leads to true happiness.

It thus seems impossible to attain real happiness and contentment in life by adhering to social conventions which disregard basic spiritual values and ethical principles. Trifonov's works continue to be part of the trend in which the everyday life of the Soviet city-dweller is depicted. His works, however, are more controversial and perhaps artistically superior to those of other Soviet writers dealing with the same subject. The popularity of Trifonov among Soviet readers can be ascribed to the controversial nature of his topics as well as to his growing mastery of the genre to which he devotes most of his time.

Trifonov does not revolutionize literature, and does not deal with sensitive political issues or criticize the Soviet system. Yet the increasing attention devoted to his works is not accidental. Urbanization has developed rapidly while the advocates of a return to the 'roots' and to the patriarchal values of the Russian countryside have been vehemently attacked.[41] It is no wonder, therefore, that the ethical values and problems of the city population have become one of the main concerns of Soviet ideologists and writers alike. One leading Soviet critic points even to a 'danger of a spiritual and ethical vacuum for man and society.'[42]

Soviet literary criticism is seriously concerned with such a situation, primarily because literature is a vehicle of ideology. Moreover, the works of writers such as Trifonov pose the problem of the ethics of the city-dweller with poignant intensity. Feliks Kuznetsov suggests in his discussion of the ethics of Soviet city life that 'according to the law of socialism the importance of the problems related to spiritual bread increases in direct proportion to the growth of the material well-being of the people.'[43] It thus appears that there is an inherent contradiction in the very process of the alleged transition from socialism to communism; a process which should be accompanied by a constant growth of material well-being and a rise in the living standard. Theoretically, a communist society could be built only on sound ethical grounds and by people selflessly devoted to their cause. The development of socialism in the Soviet Union has led instead to an increased aspiration for material satisfaction without due regard to the spiritual price which has to be paid for it.

The problems posed by the works of Trifonov are of the utmost importance to

Soviet society. It is clear that the establishment of a new social order and of a new relationship between people in the process of production does not change the very essence of man overnight; nor does it make all people within a certain system alike. They remain different, they resist change, and they are often irrational. The question then remains: how do you build a perfect and uniform society when most of its components are different and imperfect? It is indeed a challenge of almost insurmountable magnitude and it remains to be seen how it can be resolved.

Conclusion

This brief discussion of Soviet literature in the 1970s and the analysis of the work of a number of prominent writers shows that there has been during the last decade a thematic evolution in Soviet prose, prompted by changes in Soviet life. The best Soviet writers endeavour to pose in their works the monumental problems facing Soviet man and society. They search for new outlets for their creative designs in an attempt to create a new image of a man in conflict with himself and with society.

As opposed to the works appearing in the heyday of socialist realism, most of today's prose concentrates on the negative aspects of Soviet life, and writers tend to avoid suggesting solutions to the problems posed in their works. The leading Soviet writers explore the effect of technological and social progress on man and society; they investigate man's relationship to nature and to his environment; they discuss the effect of the Soviet way of life and modern conventions on the Soviet family, and, in particular, on woman's place in modern society. The main concern, however, which permeates the works of almost all the writers discussed, is the ethical foundation of Soviet man: the relation of man to man, and the spiritual values which should guide him in his actions. It appears that many writers approach the discussion of ethical problems from general, 'non-class' positions; and a number of the imperfections of Soviet man, as depicted on the pages of Soviet literature, could be attributed to the shortcomings of a system which has failed to change man in a positive sense. The lack of a positive message in many works often provokes severe attacks from official Soviet criticism.

As has been shown in the examples of Rasputin and Trifonov, writers are often called upon to interfere with the normal development of their creative process, and to give an unequivocal expression of their position in relation to their heroes, a fact which often hampers the growth of artistic talent. It is impossible to create good literature when the author must thrust his own views upon the reader. The moment literature becomes overtly didactic it ceases to be good literature.

Most Soviet prose is realistic and it has changed little in style in the last decade. The best writers try, however, to experiment by varying their narrative techniques and by introducing elements of fantasy and symbolism. Many writers resort in their works to the use of folklore, legends, and myth. There has also been an evolution in the Russian language used in Soviet literature. Most writers endeavour to use the language of the milieu depicted; they introduce a number of neologisms. Thus, the language of Rasputin is the language of the Siberian peasant, while the language of Trifonov is that of the urban intelligentsia. There has also been experimentation in the plot structure of recent works. Many writers make use of flashbacks, instant transition from the depiction of the present to the past, and the introduction of a number of different narrators.

The relation between literary theory and practice has changed greatly in the last decade. Theory is now slow in generalizing the experience of literary practice, and socialist realism has lost much of its significance as the leading 'method' of Soviet art. Instead, the implementation of the principle of *partiinost'* is continuously stressed and the importance of a work of art is often determined by its educational value which should be expressed in the affirmation of the Soviet way of life.

The situation in the past, when literary theory could prescribe how good literature was to be written, is no longer in existence. However, what theory no longer prescribes beforehand, editorial control and official criticism enforce in due course. The results are just the same. There are very few writers who can elude the vigilant eye of the censor and the editor by having a work published that is of dubious value to the Party and the Soviet state. On the rare occasions when such a work does manage to get published in a journal, it will never see the light again unless the second edition is drastically changed and the thrust of the work is altered. This process affects not only the work of individual writers but also whole literary trends whose development is not seen as being in the best interests of the immediate objectives of Soviet art.

As a result of sharp critical attacks, 'village prose' and *byt* literature have lost much of their previous significance as independent literary trends, and many writers who specialized in these fields have been driven into oblivion or forced to diversify their artistic interests by turning to a kind of literature not always suited to their creative talents. This process, which does not stimulate artistic originality and which stifles genuine artistic inspiration (which is at least partially subconscious) has had the result that much Soviet literature being produced now is mediocre and uninspiring, and most works have no mark of artistic individuality. The only positive sign and hope for the future is that there are still a number of truly gifted craftsmen who, despite all pressures on them, manage to turn out excellent works. Works such as 'Belyi parokhod' by Aitmatov or 'Poslednii srok' by Rasputin are good literature by any standards.

Notes

INTRODUCTION

1 V. Ozerov 'Na novykh rubezhakh' *Pravda* 21 Jan. 1977 3
2 Nina Podzorova 'Mesto v obshchezhitii. Zametki o proze molodykh' *Nash sovremennik* 1977 no. 7 178
3 Liliia Beliaeva 'Sem' let ne v schet' *Novyi mir* 1976 no. 4 104
4 *Literaturnaia gazeta* 16 Nov. 1977 3

1 / THE SOVIET LITERARY SCENE

1 G.N. Pospelov 'On the Controversy about the Literature of Socialist Realism' *Soviet Studies in Literature* 12 no. 1 (1975–6) 49
2 Ibid
3 Iu. Kuz'menko 'Chtob peredat' bogatstvo nashei zhizni ...' *Voprosy literatury* 1977 no. 4 51
4 'O formakh khudozhestvennogo obobshcheniia v sotsialisticheskom realizme' *Voprosy literatury* 1972 no. 1 74
5 'O nekotorykh problemakh sotsialisticheskogo realizma' *Znamia* 1975 no. 9 240
6 Ibid 241
7 A. Ovcharenko *Sotsialisticheskaia literatura i sovremennyi literaturnyi protses* (Moscow 1973) 165
8 L. Lazarev, 'I vnov' – problemy metoda' *Voprosy literatury* 1977 no. 7 22–3
9 'Vsmatrivaias' v novoe' *Voprosy literatury* 1972 no. 5 58
10 *Literaturnaia gazeta* 18 June 1975 2
11 'Kamo griadeshi?' *Novyi mir* 1970 no. 12 220–1
12 A. Metchenko 'Sotsialisticheskii realism: rasshiriaiushchiesia vozmozhnosti i teoreticheskie spory' *Oktiabr'* 1976 no. 5 191
13 A. Dubrovin 'Trebuetsia novaia smelost' ...' *Novyi mir* 1976 no. 1 230
14 L. Lazarev 'I vnov' ' 24

15 'Edinstvo khudozhestvennogo metoda i mnogoobrazie stilei v literature sotsialisticheskogo realizma' in L.G. Iakimenko ed *Ideinoe edinstvo i khudozhestvennoe mnogoobrazie sovetskoi prozy* (Moscow 1974) 9

16 'Tochka opory' *Literaturnaia gazeta* 20 Mar. 1974 2

17 L. I. Timofeev and S. V. Turaev *Slovar' literaturovedcheskikh terminov* (Moscow 1974) 234. For a detailed discussion of the principles of *ideinost'*, *klassovost'*, *narodnost'*, and *partiinost'* in art, see: N.N. Shneidman 'The Russian Classical Literary Heritage and the Basic Concepts of Soviet Literary Education' *Slavic Review* 31 (1972) 626–38.

18 L.I. Timofeev *Osnovy teorii literatury* (Moscow 1966) 124

19 *O narodnosti* (Moscow 1970) 14

20 'Obshchestvennye nauki – boevoe oruzhie partii v stroitel'stve kommunizma' *Kommunist* 1972 no. 1 27

21 'Sotsialisticheskii realizm segodnia' *Literaturnaia gazeta* 6 Feb. 1974 3

22 *Tvorcheskaia individual'nost' pisatelia i razvitie literatury* (Moscow 1970) 186

23 *Voprosy literatury* 1973 no. 2 5

24 L. Eidlin *Literaturnaia gazeta* 18 June 1975 2

25 *Voprosy literatury* 1975 no. 9 24

26 G.N. Pospelov 'Controversy' 51, 56 (emphasis in the original)

27 A. Dubrovin 'Trebuetsia' 231

28 Ibid 232

29 V.I. Lenin *Polnoe sobranie sochinenii* 39 (5th ed 1963) 152–3 (emphasis in the original)

30 G.N. Pospelov 'Controversy' 62

31 Ibid

32 Gleb Struve *Russian Literature under Lenin and Stalin 1917–1953* (Norman, Oklahoma 1971) 258

33 *Survey* 18 no. 1/82 (1972) 96

34 In the original, *Sodybų tuštejimo metas* (Vilnius 1970)

35 According to Igor Kosin, Soviet literary periodicals devote approximately 15 to 20 per cent of the total space to literature in some way related to the war. Thus, for example, in *Moskva* in 1971 – 19 per cent of the total space was devoted to the subject of war; in 1972 – 22 per cent; in *Oktiabr'* in 1971 – 21 per cent; in 1972 – 7 per cent; in *Novyi mir* in 1971 – 13 per cent; in 1972 – 16 per cent. See Igor Kosin 'The "War Theme" in Soviet Literature' *Research Studies* 41 (1973) 285.

36 In 1946, in his novel *V okopakh Stalingrada*, Viktor Nekrasov started a new trend in war literature by exposing the truth about the difficulties and horrors of everyday life at the front. In the days of Stalin, however, Nekrasov had few followers. In 1961 Bulat Okudzhava published the story 'Bud' zdorov shkoliar' ' in which he portrays the fear and anguish of an inexperienced teenage boy who is totally unprepared for war, and who is not afraid to admit that he wants to live and fears death. See K. Paustovskii ed *Tarusskie tetradi* (Kaluga 1961) 50–75.

37 For a detailed discussion of Soviet 'village prose,' see Geoffrey A. Hosking 'The Russian Peasant Rediscovered: "Village Prose" of the 1960s' *Slavic Review* 32 (1973) 705–24; Gleb Žekulin 'The Contemporary Countryside in Soviet Literature: A Search for New Values' in James R. Millar ed *The Soviet Rural Community* (Urbana 1971) 376–404

38 *Literaturnaia gazeta* 12 Nov. 1975 1. *Priasliny* is a trilogy which includes *Brat'ia i sestry* (Brothers and Sisters) (1958), *Dve zimy i tri leta* (Two Winters and Three Summers) (1968), and *Puti – pereput'ia* (Ways of the Byways) (1973).

39 For a discussion of the growing interest in the Russian past and the alleged return to 'roots,' see *Slavic Review* 32 (1973) 1–44.

40 'Protiv antiistorizma' *Literaturnaia gazeta* 15 Nov. 1972 5

41 E. Starikova 'Sotsiologicheskii aspekt "derevenskoi prozy"' *Voprosy literatury* 1972 no. 7 12. The views expressed here by E. Starikova are shared by many other Soviet critics and writers. At a meeting held at the Writers' Union in September 1978 to discuss the perspectives of 'village prose' different speakers reaffirmed Starikova's views by asserting that too many writers prefer to write about the difficult past of the Soviet countryside, devoting at the same time little attention to the Soviet village of the 1970s, particularly to the life of the *sovkhoz* (Soviet farm) workers. The main speaker at this meeting, L. Novichenko, stated unequivocally that 'the main position in the literature of socialist realism should be occupied by a socially active hero who grows and develops in step with his growing contribution to the peoples' cause.' See 'Gorizonty "derevenskoi prozy"' *Literaturnaia gazeta* 27 Sept. 1978 2.

42 E. Starikova 'Aspekt' 35

43 Ibid 27

44 *Sever* 1966 no. 1, republished as a book in 1967 in Moscow

45 P.S. Vykhodtsev ed *Kurs lektsii po istorii sotsialisticheskogo realizma* (Moscow 1973) 98

46 *Literaturnaia gazeta* 24 Dec. 1975 7

47 *Novyi mir* 1975 no. 4 11–113, no. 5 118–70, and no. 6 83–118

48 *Nash sovremennik* 1977 no. 4 15–86, and no. 5 19–65

49 *Lipiagi* (Moscow 1967)

50 *Moskva* 1968 no. 10 52–186

51 *Kresty* in *Moskva* 1975 no. 7 3–101 and no. 8 45–103; *Okruzhenie* in *Nash sovremennik* 1976 no. 11 70–129 and no. 12 15–114

52 Sergei Krutilin 'Proshchaias's geroem' *Literaturnaia gazeta* 4 May 1977 3

53 *Nash sovremennik* 1978 no. 3 3–90

54 The final chapters of 'Poslednii poklon' have been published in *Nash sovremennik* 1978 no. 1 3–105.

55 'Pastukh i pastushka. Sovremennaia pastoral'' *Nash sovremennik* 1971 no. 8 2–70

56 'Tsar'-ryba. Povestvovanie v rasskazakh,' *Nash sovremennik* 1976 no. 4 3–81, no. 5 22–91, and no. 6 6–78

57 *Novyi mir* 1973 no. 1 118–71

58 *Nash sovremennik* 1973 no. 2 3–80

59 *Novyi mir* 1974 no. 9 82–130

60 *Novyi mir* 1977 no. 1 11–76

61 *Druzhba narodov* 1977 no. 5 15–150

62 Ibid 150

63 *Novyi mir* 1977 no. 4 7–80, no. 5 21–105, and no. 6 8–127

64 *Novyi mir* 1975 no. 2 26–97, and no. 3 19–89

65 *Novyi mir* 1970 no. 12 101–40

66 *Novyi mir* 1971 no. 8 53–107

67 *Druzhba narodov* 1973 no. 1 76–118, and no. 2 63–93

68 *Nash sovremennik* 1973 no. 1 3–79, and no. 2 81–139

69 *Znamia* 1973 no. 3 58–118

70 *Neva* 1973 no. 1 140–69

71 For a discussion of Soviet *byt* literature, see N.N. Shneidman 'The Controversial Prose of the 1970's: Problems of Marriage and Love in Contemporary Soviet Literature' *Canadian Slavonic Papers* 18 (1976) 400–14.

72 L. Iakimenko 'Ispytanie chuvstvom? ...' *Voprosy literatury* 1973 no. 9 37

73 V. Perevedentsev 'Varianty' *Literaturnoe obozrenie* 1973 no. 5 32–8. According to Perevedentsev, the social structures and schemes created, for example, in Zalygin's novel *Iuzhno-amerikanskii variant*, are very realistic (see discussion in ch. 4). To substantiate such allegations he quotes statistical data according to which for every 1,000 marriages in major Soviet cities, there are close to 500 divorces. In Moscow, where the action of the novel takes place, the number reaches 535.

74 *Novyi mir* 1973 no. 7 4–61, and no. 8 101–51

75 *Teatr* 1973 no. 4 138–68

76 *Nash sovremennik* 1972 no. 3 2–33

77 'Korni i pobegi' *Literaturnaia gazeta* 9 Mar. 1977 5

78 'Samosoznanie iskusstva' *Novyi mir* 1976 no. 10 256

79 'Obraz geroia – obraz vremeni' *Literaturnaia gazeta* 20 July 1977 5

80 *Novyi mir* 1977 no. 2 14–127, and no. 3 27–108

81 Viacheslav Shugaev '... obreteniia v itoge' *Literaturnaia gazeta* 15 June 1977 5

82 Oleg Salynskii 'Poteri v puti?' *Literaturnaia gazeta* 15 June 1977 5

83 *Novyi mir* 1974 no. 3 17–100, and no. 4 100–68

84 *Znamia* 1976 no. 1 32–84, and no. 2 37–88

85 Viktor Astaf'ev 'Peresekaia rubezh' interview with Al. Mikhailov *Voprosy literatury* 1974 no. 11 218

86 E. Sidorov 'Prodolzhenie sleduet' *Voprosy literatury* 1976 no. 6 34

2 / CHINGIZ AITMATOV

1 VI. Voronov *Chingiz Aitmatov. Ocherk tvorchestva* (Moscow 1976) 15

2 Ibid 16. For a discussion of Aitmatov's early works and an interview with him see *Russian Literature Triquarterly* 16 (1979) 244–68.

3 *Novyi mir* 1958 no. 8 3–31

4 *Novyi mir* 1966 no. 3 9–99

5 *Novyi mir* 1970 no. 1 31–100

6 *Novyi mir* 1975 no. 9 37–94

7 *Znamia* 1977 no. 4 4–55

8 *The Ascent of Mount Fuji* bilingual edition, tr Nicholas Bethell (New York 1975)

9 Chingiz Aitmatov 'Tochka prisoedineniia' interview with V. Levchenko *Voprosy literatury* 1976 no. 8 156

10 *Oktiabr'* 1958 no. 3 131–55 (appeared in the original Kirghiz in June 1957)
11 *Nash sovremennik* 1974 no. 10 2–88, and no. 11 58–91
12 Chingiz Aitmatov *Povesti i rasskazy* (Moscow 1970) 440–516
13 *Novyi mir* 1962 no. 7 3–33
14 *Novyi mir* 1963 no. 5 6–61
15 *Novyi mir* 1961 no. 2 54–74
16 'Tochka prisoedineniia' 166
17 VI. Voronov *Aitmatov* 184
18 On 7 April 1976 I had an opportunity to meet Chingiz Aitmatov and to discuss with him problems of Soviet literature in general and of his creative activity in particular. All references to Aitmatov's views unless otherwise indicated are taken from these discussions which took place in the House of the Writers' Creative Activity in Peredelkino, near Moscow.
19 In the book form edition Chingiz Aitmatov *Povesti i rasskazy* (Moscow 1970) 'Posle skazki' appears in the title and 'Belyi parokhod' in parentheses. Aitmatov claims that he prefers the title 'Posle skazki' while Aleksandr Tvardovskii, the editor of *Novyi mir*, who accepted the story for publication, preferred the title 'Belyi parokhod.' See *Voprosy literatury* 1976 no. 8 158.
20 'Tochka prisoedineniia' 156
21 Ibid 153
22 Ibid 150
23 'Skazki pishut dlia khrabrykh' *Literaturnaia gazeta* 1 July 1970 5 (emphasis in the original)
24 Ibid
25 'Ne skazkoi edinoi ...' *Literaturnaia gazeta* 1 July 1970 5
26 Ibid (emphasis in the original)
27 'Kak cheloveku chelovekom byt'' *Iunost'* 1973 no. 5 68
28 Ibid
29 'Neobkhodimye utochneniia' *Literaturnaia gazeta* 29 July 1970 4
30 Ibid
31 Ibid
32 'Tochka prisoedineniia' 166
33 '"Krasnoe iabloko" i "Belyi parohkod" ...' *Literaturnaia gazeta* 2 July 1975 8
34 'Tochka prisoedineniia' 146–7
35 *Literaturnaia gazeta* 29 July 1970 4
36 *Znamia* 1977 no. 4 11
37 Ibid 37
38 See among others A. Kondratovich 'Muza v tumane' *Literaturnaia gazeta* 12 Apr. 1978 5.
39 'Kirpichnoe mirozdanie ili energiia mifa' *Literaturnaia gazeta* 29 Mar. 1978 5
40 Ibid
41 *The Ascent of Mount Fuji* 184
42 From a speech delivered at the Plenary Session of the Boards of the Creative Unions of the USSR (*Literaturnaia gazeta* 17 Dec. 1969 5)
43 Ibid

3 / BONDAREV AND BYKOV

1 For a discussion of the recent critical literature dealing with the subject of war in Soviet literature see N. Ermolaeva and P. Kuprianovskii 'V razdum'iakh o literature i voine' *Voprosy literatury* 1976 no. 6 218–35.

2 See Iurii Bondarev *Poisk istiny* (Moscow 1976) 148–64.

3 The most important novels and novellas by Iurii Bondarev dealing with the war are: 'Iunost' Komandirov' (1956); 'Batal'ony prosiat ognia' (1957); 'Poslednie zalpy' (1959); *Tishina* (1962); *Goriachii sneg* (1969); *Bereg* (1975). Vasil' Bykov's war stories include: 'Zhuravlinyi krik' (1960); 'Tret'ia raketa' (1961); 'Al'piiskaia ballada' (1963); 'Mertvym ne bol'no' (1966); 'Ataka s khodu' (1968); 'Kruglianskii most' (1969); 'Sotnikov' (1970); 'Obelisk' (1972); 'Dozhit' do rassveta' (1972); 'Volch'ia staia' (1974); 'Ego batal'on' (1976); 'Poiti i ne vernut'sia' (1978).

4 A. Bocharov 'Spor prodolzhaetsia i segodnia' *Druzhba narodov* 1966 no. 5 283

5 Vasil' Bykov *Povesti* (Moscow 1975) 19–128

6 *Novyi mir* 1968 no. 5 10–71

7 Ibid 59

8 *Novyi mir* 1966 no. 1 3–66 and no. 2 7–64

9 *Novyi mir* 1970 no. 5 65–161

10 A. Bocharov 'Spor prodolzhaestia i segodnia,' 283

11 Vasil' Bykov *Povesti* 317–447

12 Ibid 129–248

13 Vasil' Bykov 'Velikaia akademiia – zhizn' ' interview with L. Lazarev *Voprosy literatury* 1975 no. 1 130

14 'Kruglianskii most' *Novyi Mir* 1969 no. 3 3–57; 'Sotnikov'; 'Obelisk' *Novyi mir* 1972 no. 1 3–44; 'Volch'ia staia' *Novyi mir* 1974 no. 7 5–80; 'Poiti i ne vernut'sia' *Neva* 1978 no. 5 19–115

15 Oleg Mikhailov 'Preodolenie' *Nash sovremennik* 1974 no. 6 176–80

16 *Nash sovremennik* 1976 no. 1 12–120

17 L. Lazarev 'Silami strelkovogo batal'ona' *Druzhba narodov* 1976 no. 9 269

18 *Poisk istiny* 37

19 In English translation: *Silence* tr Elizaveta Fen (London 1965). The novel was originally published in two parts. In part one the action takes place in 1945, and in part two in 1949. In Bondarev's *Sobranie sochinenii v chetyrekh tomakh* 2 (Moscow 1973), the novel has three parts, the last part being previously published as a separate story under the title 'Dvoe.' The action in part three takes place in 1953, and the main protagonists are Sergei's sister Asia and her husband Kostia.

20 *Silence* 242

21 Mikhail Kuznetsov 'Ispoved' pokolenia' in Iurii Bondarev *Sobranie sochinenii v chetyrekh tomakh* 1 (Moscow 1973) 37

22 *Znamia* 1969 no. 9 3–51, no. 10 5–110, and no. 11 7–90

23 Iurii Bondarev *Sobranie sochinenii v chetyrekh tomakh* 3 (Moscow 1973) 95

24 'Iunost' komandirov' (1956), 'Batal'ony prosiat ognia' (1957), 'Poslednie zalpy' (1959)

25 *Nash sovremennik* 1975 no. 3 2–87, no. 4 8–113, no. 5 47–114
26 Al'bert Likhanov 'Neodnoznachnost' glubiny' *Voprosy literatury* 1975 no. 9 63.
Likhanov's view is shared by a number of Soviet critics.
27 Iurii Bondarev 'Chelovek neset v sebe mir ...' *Literaturnaia gazeta* 30 Mar. 1977 4
28 Ibid
29 I. Zhukov 'I nakhodia istinu v poiske' *Voprosy literatury* 1976 no. 3 62
30 A. Bocharov 'Vremia kristallizatsii' *Voprosy literatury* 1976 no. 3 34

4 / SERGEI ZALYGIN

1 For a biographical sketch see Galina Kolesnikova *Sergei Zalygin. Tvorcheskaia biografiia* (Moscow 1969).
2 Sergei Zalygin 'Zamysel, rabota, proizvedenie' *Voprosy literatury* 1973 no. 4 157–8
3 L. Terakopian *Sergei Zalygin. Pisatel' i geroi* (Moscow 1973) 14–16
4 *Novyi mir* 1954 no. 8 3–55. In the book edition the title reads *Vesnoi 1954 goda*.
5 *Novyi mir* 1956 no. 7 44–85
6 Sergei Zalygin *Izbrannye proizvedeniia v dvukh tomakh* 1 (Moscow 1973) 541
7 *Novyi mir* 1962 no. 1 3–77, no. 2 65–131, and no. 3 49–129
8 For a discussion of Zalygin's works of the 1960s see N.N. Shneidman 'A New Approach to Old Problems: The Contemporary Prose of Sergej Zalygin' *Russian Language Journal* 30 no. 106 (1976) 115–29.
9 *Novyi mir* 1964 no. 2 3–80
10 *Novyi mir* 1967 no. 4 3–94, no. 5 22–89, and no. 6 5–116
11 Zalygin's observations on his creative work related in this chapter, unless quoted from other sources, are taken from my conversation with the writer held on 1 April 1976 in Moscow.
12 L. Terakopian *Zalygin* 71
13 *Nash sovremennik* 1973 no. 1 2–79, and no. 2 80–139
14 Vera Smirnova 'Lichnaia zhizn' inzhenera Mansurovoi' *Literaturnaia Rossiia* 20 Apr. 1973 10 and 13
15 *Literaturnye zaboty* (Moscow 1972) 17–19
16 'Nesostoiashchiisia variant' *Oktiabr'* 1973 no. 8 201. For a detailed discussion of *Iuzhno-amerikanskii variant* and the Soviet *byt* literature of the early 1970s, see N.N. Shneidman 'The Controversial Prose of the 1970's: Problems of Marriage and Love in Contemporary Soviet Literature.'
17 'Ispytanie fantaziei' *Literaturnaia Rossiia* 29 June 1973 6
18 *Literaturnye zaboty* 64
19 *Druzhba narodov* 1973 no. 9 3–99
20 Ibid 4
21 *Nash sovremennik* 1975 no. 9 11–111, no. 10 44–121, and no. 11 13–105
22 Sergei Zalygin *Izbrannye proizvedeniia v dvukh tomakh* 2 395
23 *Nash sovremennik* 1975 no. 10 119
24 V. Baranov 'Novye dali tvorchestva' *Voprosy literatury* 1976 no. 6 21

25 Valerii Dement'ev 'Zvezdy ochnulis' ...' *Literaturnaia gazeta* 28 Jan. 1976 4
26 Ibid
27 'Dukhu Khel'sinki alternativy net' *Literaturnaia gazeta* 22 June 1977 3
28 *Literaturnye zaboty* 12
29 Ibid 11–13

5 / VALENTIN RASPUTIN

1 Valentin Rasputin 'Byt' samim soboi' interview with Evg. Osetrov *Voprosy literatury* 1976 no. 9 142
2 Valentin Rasputin *Krai vozle samogo neba* Vostochno-sibirskoe knizhnoe izdatel'stvo 1966. Reviewed by V. Turbin in *Druzhba narodov* 1967 no. 12 274–5. The reviewer rates Rasputin's sketches very highly. He claims that even on the basis of this single work the young writer could become the leader of all writers who are concerned with the relationship of man and nature.
3 (Krasnoiarsk 1967)
4 *Almanakh: Angara* 1967 no. 4, and *Sibirskie ogni* 1967 no. 9
5 See *Zhivi i pomni. Povesti i rasskazy* (Moscow 1975) 195–208 and 209–20.
6 'Den'gi dlia Marii' in *Vniz i vverkh po techeniu. Povesti* (Moscow 1972) 211
7 *Nash sovremennik* 1970 no. 7 3–53, and no. 8 8–54
8 'Tortilla Flat' in *The Short Novels of John Steinbeck* (New York 1953) 128
9 *Literaturnaia gazeta* 6 June 1973 4
10 O. Salynskii 'Dom i dorogi' *Voprosy literatury* 1977 no. 2 9
11 Ibid 15
12 'Srok svershenii' *Literaturnaia gazeta* 10 Dec. 1975 5
13 'Zametki o iazyke sovremennoi prozy' *Novyi mir* 1972 no. 1 232
14 *Nash sovremennik* 1974 no. 10 2–88, and no. 11 58–91
15 *Oktiabr'* 1958 no. 3 131–55. It appeared in the original Kirghiz in June 1957.
16 *Nash sovremennik* 1976 no. 10 3–71, and no. 11 17–64
17 See ch. 1 note 37.
18 *Nash sovremennik* 1972 no. 6 3–39
19 'Ne mog ne prostit'sia s Materoi' *Literaturnaia gazeta* 16 Mar. 1977 3
20 Iu. Seleznev 'Zemlia ili territoriia?' *Voprosy literatury* 1977 no. 2 56
21 *Nash sovremennik* 1976 no. 10 43
22 'Ne mog ne prostit'sia s Materoi' 3
23 Ibid
24 'Byt' samim soboi' 145
25 'Vasilii i Vasilisa' in *Zhivi i pomni* 221–42
26 'Byt' samim soboi' 149
27 Ibid 150
28 'Grazhdanstvennost' pozitsii' *Literaturnaia gazeta* 23 Mar. 1977 4
29 O. Salynskii 'Dom i dorogi' 33
30 *Voprosy literatury* 1977 no. 2 80
31 Ibid

32 *Literaturnaia gazeta* 6 June 1973 4
33 'Preodolevaia zabvenie' *Literaturnaia gazeta* 26 Jan. 1977 5
34 'Byt' samim soboi' 146
35 'Ne mog ne prostit'sia s Materoi' 3
36 See Sergei Zalygin 'Srok svershenii' *Literaturnaia gazeta* 10 Dec. 1975 5. In my conversation with Sergei Zalygin in Moscow in April 1976, Zalygin praised Rasputin and spoke of his creative work with admiration.
37 'Ne mog ne prostit'sia s Materoi' 3

6 / IURII TRIFONOV

1 *Novyi mir* 1950 no. 10 56–175, and no. 11 49–182. This novel was subsequently republished as a book in Moscow in 1952.
2 *Znamia* 1963 no. 4 81–118, no. 5 3–39, no. 6 3–68, and no. 7 3–88. This was republished as a book in 1963 in Moscow.
3 'Vera i Zoika' and 'Byl letnii polden' ' *Novyi mir* 1966 no. 12 75–85 and 85–91
4 *Novyi mir* 1968 no. 8 67–75
5 *Novyi mir* 1969 no. 12 29–65
6 *Novyi mir* 1970 no. 12 101–40
7 *Novyi mir* 1971 no. 8 53–107
8 *Novyi mir* 1975 no. 8 7–99
9 *Druzhba narodov* 1976 no. 1 83–167
10 *Druzhba narodov* 1978 no. 3 27–153
11 For a description of the relationship between Trifonov and Tvardovskii, see Iurii Trifonov 'Zapiski soseda. Iz vospominanii' in *Prodolzhitel'nye uroki* (Moscow 1975) 27–66.
12 *Znamia* 1965 no. 2 142–60, and no. 3 152–77
13 *Novyi mir* 1973 no. 3 44–116, no. 4 35–112, and no. 5 8–90
14 *Novyi mir* 1969 no. 12 64
15 'Utverzhdenie nravstvennosti' Introduction to Iurii Trifonov *Rasskazy i povesti* (Moscow 1971) 8
16 Ibid
17 On 16 April 1976 I had an opportunity to meet Iurii Trifonov and to discuss with him the problems of Soviet literature in general and of his own creative activity in particular. All references to Trifonov's views, unless otherwise indicated, are taken from these discussions which took place in the writer's Moscow apartment.
18 *Novyi mir* 1975 no. 8 31
19 Ibid 95
20 Ibid 24
21 *Novyi mir* 1970 no. 12 123
22 'Sovremennost' – splav istorii i budushchego' *Literaturnaia gazeta* 19 June 1974 6
23 *Prodolzhitel'nye uroki* 95
24 Ibid 8
25 Ibid 26
26 Ibid 5 (emphasis in the original)

27 L. Fink 'Zybkost' kharaktera ili zybkost' zamysla' *Literaturnaia gazeta* 29 Oct. 1975 4

28 'Prokrustovo lozhe byta' *Literaturnaia gazeta* 12 May 1976 4 (emphasis in the original)

29 *Literaturnaia gazeta* 23 June 1976 2

30 *Literaturnaia gazeta* 30 June 1976 4

31 Iurii Trifonov 'Vybirat', reshat'sia, zhertvovat'' *Voprosy literatury* 1972 no. 2 63–4

32 See, among others, 'Pogovorim o strannostiakh liubvi' in *Voprosy literatury* 1973 no. 9 19–100.

33 *Novyi mir* 1975 no. 8 50

34 'Voskhozhdenie' *Oktiabr'* 1975 no. 8 208 (emphasis in the original)

35 'Ispytanie posredstvennosti: nekotorye itogi' *Voprosy literatury* 1972 no. 2 61

36 Trifonov *Students* (Moscow 1953) 10

37 *Voprosy literatury* 1972 no. 2 64

38 Ibid

39 Ibid

40 For a discussion of the above, see Geoffrey Hosking 'The Search for an Image of Man in Contemporary Soviet Fiction' *Forum of Modern Language Studies* 11 (1975) 349–65.

41 A. Iakovlev 'Protiv antiistorizma' *Literaturnaia gazeta* 15 Nov. 1972 4–5

42 Feliks Kuznetsov 'Dukhovnye tsennosti: mify i deistvitel'nost'' *Novyi mir* 1974 no. 1 213

43 'Literatura zrelogo sotsializma' *Literaturnaia gazeta* 5 Nov. 1975 4

Selected Bibliography

It would be impossible to give here an exhaustive list of monographs and articles dealing with the development of Soviet literature, and it is not necessary for this study. The list of suggested background reading is therefore limited to several Soviet and Western histories of literature, and a number of books and articles in which different aspects of the theory and practice of Soviet literature are discussed.

The list of Soviet prose in the 1970s includes a number of works by leading Soviet authors, officially published in the USSR, representing different thematic and artistic trends. This list includes also works published prior to 1970 by writers to whom separate chapters are devoted in this book.

The list of Soviet prose in English translation is limited to works by writers discussed in chapters two to six.

BACKGROUND READING

Brown, Deming B. *Soviet Russian Literature Since Stalin* Cambridge 1978

Brown, E.J. *Russian Literature Since the Revolution* New York 1963

Bullitt, Margaret M. 'Towards a Marxist Theory of Aesthetics: The Development of Socialist Realism in the Soviet Union' *Russian Review* 35 (1976) 53–76

Demaite, Ann 'The Great Debate on Socialist Realism' *The Modern Language Journal* 50 (1966) 263–8

Dementev, A.G. ed *Istoriia russkoi sovetskoi literatury v 4-kh tomakh. 1917–1965* Moscow 1967–71

Dunham, Vera S. *In Stalin's Time: Middleclass Values in Soviet Fiction* Cambridge 1976

Ermolaev, Herman *Soviet Literary Theories 1917–1934: The Genesis of Socialist Realism* Berkeley 1963

Gasiorowska, Xenia 'On Happiness in Recent Soviet Fiction' *Russian Literature Triquarterly* no. 9 (1974) 473–85

– 'Two Decades of Love and Marriage in Soviet Fiction' *Russian Review* 34 (1975) 10–21

Gibian, George 'The Urban Theme in Recent Soviet Russian Prose: Notes Towards a Typology' *Slavic Review* 37 (1978) 40–50

Hayward, Max 'The Decline of Socialist Realism' *Survey* 18 (1972) 73–97

Hayward, Max and Edward L. Crowley eds *Soviet Literature in the Sixties. An International Symposium* New York 1964

Hayward, Max and Leopold Labedz *Literature and Revolution in Soviet Russia 1917–1962* London 1963

Hosking, Geoffrey A. 'The Russian Peasant Rediscovered: "Village Prose" of the 1960s' *Slavic Review* 32 (1973) 705–24

– 'The Search for an Image of Man in Contemporary Soviety Fiction' *Forum for Modern Language Studies* 11 (1975) 349–65

Iakimenko, L.G. ed *Ideinoe edinstvo i khudozhestvennoe mnogoobrazie sovetskoi prozy* Moscow 1974

Ivanov, V. *Ideino-esteticheskie printsipy sovetskoi literatury* 2nd ed Moscow 1975

James, C.V. *Soviet Socialist Realism; Origins and Theory* London 1973

Johnson, Priscilla *Krushchev and the Arts. The Politics of Soviet Culture 1962–1964* Cambridge, Mass. 1965

Khrapchenko, M. *The Writer's Creative Individuality and the Development of Literature* Moscow 1977

Labedz, Leopold 'The Destiny of Writers in Revolutionary Movements' *Survey* 18 (1972) 8–46

Markov, D. *Problemy teorii sotsialisticheskogo realizma* Moscow 1975

– 'Sovremennyi etap teorii sotsialisticheskogo realizma (Razmyshleniia o dostignutom, o novykh problemakh)' *Znamia* 1978 no. 5 201–10

Ovcharenko, A. *Sotsialisticheskaia literatura i sovremennyi literaturnyi protsess* 2nd ed Moscow 1975

Petrov, S.M. *Osnovnye voprosy teorii realizma. Kriticheskii realizm. Sotsialisticheskii realizm* Moscow 1975

Pospelov, G.N. 'On the Controversy about the Literature of Socialist Realism' *Soviet Studies in Literature* 12 (1975–6) 48–70

Schneidman, N.N. 'The Controversial Prose of the 1970's: Problems of Marriage and Love in Contemporary Soviet Literature' *Canadian Slavonic Papers* 18 (1976) 400–14

– Interview with Chingiz Aitmatov *Russian Literature Triquarterly* 16 (1979) 264–8

– 'Iurii Trifonov and the Ethics of Contemporary Soviet City Life' *Canadian Slavonic Papers* 19 (1977) 335–51

Slonim, Marc *Soviet Russian Literature. Writers and Problems 1917–1977* 2nd ed New York 1977

Struve, Gleb *Russian Literature under Lenin and Stalin 1917–1953* Norman, Oklahoma 1971

Suchkov, Boris *Istoricheskie sud'by realizma* 2nd ed Moscow 1975

Terakopian, L. *Sergei Zalygin. Pisatel' i geroi* Moscow 1973

Trifonov, Iurii *Prodolzhitel'nye uroki* Moscow 1975

Voronov, Vl. *Chingiz Aitmatov. Ocherk tvorchestva* Moscow 1976

Žekulin, Gleb 'The Contemporary Countryside in Soviet Literature: A Search for New Values' in James R. Millar ed *The Soviet Rural Community* Urbana 1971

RUSSIAN SOVIET PROSE IN THE 1970S

Abramov, Fedor *Priasliny* (1958–73): *Brat'ia i sestry* (1958), *Dve zimy i tri leta* (1968), *Puti-pereput'ia* (1973) (The Priaslins: Brothers and Sisters, Two Winters and Three Summers, Ways of the Byways)
    'Al'ka' (1972) (Al'ka)
    Dom (1978) (The House)
Aitmatov, Chingiz 'Ashim' (1954)
    'Sypaichi' (1954) (Sypaichi)
    'Belyi dozhd' ' (1955) (White Rain)
    'Soperniki' (1955) (Rivals)
    'Trudnaia pereprava' (1956) (The Difficult Crossing)
    'Litsom k litsu' (1957) (Face to Face)
    'Dzhamilia' (1958) (Dzhamilia)
    'Topolek moi v krasnoi kosynke' (1961) (To Have and to Lose)
    'Verbliuzhii glaz' (1961) (A Camel's Eye)
    'Pervyi uchitel' ' (1962) (The First Teacher)
    'Materinskoe pole' (1963) (Mother Earth)
    'Proshchai, Gul'sary!' (1966) (Farewell, Gul'sary!)
    'Belyi parokhod (Posle skazki)' (1970) (The White Steamship)
    'Rannie zhuravli' (1975) (Early Cranes)
    'Pegii pes, begushchii kraem moria' (1977) (Spotted Dog by the Sea's Edge)
Aksenov, Vasilii 'Poiski zhanra' (1978) (In Search of a Genre)
Aleksin, Anatolii *Tretii v piatom riadu. Povesti i rasskazy* (1977) (The Third in the Fifth Row. Novelettes and stories)
Anan'ev, Anatolii *Versty liubvi* (1971) (Miles of Love)
    Gody bez voiny (1975) (Years without War)
Astaf'ev, Viktor 'Pastukh i pastushka. Sovremennaia pastoral' ' (1971) (The Shepherd and the Shepherdess)
    Poslednii poklon (1957–78) (The Last Respects)
    'Tsar'-ryba' (1976) (The King of the Fish)
Avdeenko, Aleksandr *V pote litsa svoego* ... (1978) (In the Sweat of One's Face ...)
Avyžius, Jonas *Poteriannyi krov* (1972) (The Lost Shelter)
Baklanov, Grigorii *Druz'ia* (1975) (Friends)
Belov, Vasilii *Sel'skie povesti* (1971) (Village Stories)
Bitov, Andrei *Dni cheloveka* (1976) (A Man's Days. Novelettes)
Bondarev, Iurii 'Iunost' komandirov' (1956) (The Youth of Commanders)
    'Batal'ony prosiat ognia' (1957) (The Battalions are Asking for Fire)
    'Poslednie zalpy' (1959) (The Last Volleys)
    Tishina (1962) (Silence)
    Goriachii sneg (1969) (The Hot Snow)
    Bereg (1975) (The Shore)
Bykov, Vasil' 'Zhuravlinyi krik' (1960) (The Shout of the Cranes)
    'Tret'ia raketa' (1961) (The Third Flare)

'Al'piiskaia ballada' (1963) (Alpine Ballad)
'Mertvym ne bol'no' (1966) (The Dead Feel No Pain)
'Ataka s khodu' (1968) (Full Speed Attack)
'Kruglianskii most' (1969) (The Krugliany Bridge)
'Sotnikov' (1970) (Sotnikov)
'Obelisk' (1972) (Obelisk)
'Dozhit do rassveta' (1972) (To Survive till Dawn)
'Volch'ia staia' (1974) (The Wolf Pack)
'Ego batal'on' (1976) (His Battalion)
'Poiti i ne vernut'sia' (1978) (The Road with No Return)
Chakovskii, Aleksandr *Blokada* (1969–75) (Blockade)
Granin, Daniil *Dozhd' v chuzhom gorode. Povesti* (1977) (Rain in a Strange Town. Novelettes and stories)
Iskander, Fazil' *Sandro iz Chegema* (1973) (Sandro from Chegem)
Kashtanov, Arnol'd 'Zavadskoi raion' (1973) (The Factory District)
Kolesnikov, Mikhail *Industrial'naia ballada* (1972) (Industrial Ballad)
    Izotopy dlia Altunina (1974) (Isotopes for Altunin)
    Altunin prinimaet reshenie (1976) (Altunin Makes a Decision)
    Shkola ministrov (1977) (A School for Ministers)
Krivonosov, Anatolii 'Gori, gori iasno' (1974) (Burn, Burn Brightly)
Kron, Aleksandr *Bessonitsa* (1977) (Insomnia)
Krutilin, Sergei 'Pustoshel' ' (1973) (Weeds)
    Kresty (1975) (Kresty)
    Okruzhenie (1976) (The Encirclement)
    'Masterskaia v glukhom pereulke' (1978) (A Studio in the By-Street)
Lipatov, Vil' *I eto vse o nem ...* (1974) (And All This Is about Him ...)
    Igor' Savvovich (1977) (Igor' Savvovich)
    'Povest' bez nazvaniia, siuzheta i kontsa ... ' (1978) (A Tale without a Title, Plot or Ending ...)
Likhonosov, Viktor *Elegiia. Povesti i rasskazy* (1976) (Elegy. Novelettes and stories)
Nagibin, Iurii *Ty budesh' zhit'. Povesti i rasskazy* (1974) (You Will Live. Novelettes and stories)
Nemchenko, Garii *Schitannye dni* (1974) (Numbered Days)
Nosov, Evgenii 'Usviatskie shlemonostsy' (1977) (The Helmet Bearers from Usviaty)
Prilezhaeva, Mariia 'Osen' ' (1977) (Autumn)
Proskurin, Petr *Sud'ba* (1972) (Fate)
    Imia tvoe (1977) (Your Name)
Rasputin, Valentin 'Den'gi dlia Marii' (1967) (Money for Mariia)
    'Poslednii srok' (1970) (The Final Term)
    'Vniz i vverkh po techeniiu' (1972) (Up and Down the River)
    'Zhivi i pomni' (1974) (Live and Remember)
    'Proshchanie s Materoi' (1976) (Parting with Matera)
Semin, Vitalii *Zhenia i Valentina* (1971) (Zhenia and Valentina)
Shukshin, Vasilii 'Kalina krasnaia' (1973) (The Red Snowballtree)
    Izbrannye proizvedeniia v dvukh tomakh (1975) (Collected Works in Two Volumes)

Simonov, Konstantin *Zhivye i mertvye* (1959–71): *Zhivye i mertvye* (1959), *Soldatami ne rozhdaiutsia* (1964), *Poslednee leto* (1971) (The Living and the Dead: The Living and the Dead, Men Are Not Born Soldiers, The Last Summer)

Skalon, Andrei 'Zhivye den'gi' (1972) (Ready Cash)

Skop, Iurii *Tekhnika bezopasnosti* (1977) (Safety Precautions)

Soloukhin, Vladimir *Izbrannye proizvedeniia v dvukh tomakh* (1974) (Collected works in two volumes)
  Prekrasnaia Adygené. Povesti i rasskazy (1976) (The Beautiful Adygené. Novelettes and stories)

Stadniuk, Ivan *Voina* (1974) (War)

Tendriakov, Vladimir 'Vesennie perevertyshi' (1973) (Spring Turn-Overs)
  'Tri meshka sornoi pshenitsy' (1973) (Three Bags of Weedy Wheat)
  'Noch' posle vypuska' (1974) (The Night After Graduation)
  'Zatmenie' (1977) (Eclipse)

Trifonov, Iurii *Studenty* (1950) (Students)
  Utolenie zhazhdy (1963) (The Quenching of Thirst)
  Otblesk kostra (1965) (Reflection of a Bonfire)
  'Obmen' (1969) (The Exchange)
  'Predvaritel'nye itogi' (1970) (Preliminary Results)
  'Dolgoe proshchanie' (1971) (The Long Goodbye)
  Neterpenie (1973) (Impatience)
  'Drugaia zhizn'' (1975) (Another Life)
  'Dom na naberezhnoi' (1976) (The House on the Embankment)
  Starik (1978) (The Old Man)

Vasil'ev, Boris *Ne streliaite v belykh lebedei* (1973) (Do Not Shoot the White Swans)
  V spiskakh ne znachilsia (1974) (Not Listed in the Rolls)

Velembovskaia, Irina *Tretii Semestr. Povesti* (1973) (The Third Term. Novelettes)

Zalygin, Sergei *Rasskazy* (1941) (Stories)
  Severnye rasskazy (1947) (Stories of the North)
  'Vesnoi nyneshnego goda' (1954) (In the Spring of this Year)
  'Svideteli' (1956) (Witnesses)
  Tropy Altaia (1962) (The Altai Paths)
  'Na Irtyshe' (1964) (By the Irtysh)
  Solenaia Pad' (1967) (Salt Valley)
  'Os'ka-smeshnoi mal'chik' (1973) (Os'ka the Funny Boy)
  Iuzhno-amerikanskii variant (1973) (South-American Variant)
  Komissiia (1975) (The Commission)

SOVIET WRITERS IN ENGLISH TRANSLATION

Aitmatov, Chingiz 'The Camel's Eye' *Soviet Literature* 1962 no. 7 56–79
– 'The Early Cranes' *Soviet Literature* 1976 no. 5 3–77
– *Farewell, Gul'sary!* Tr John French. London 1970
– 'Points of Contact' *Soviet Literature* 1977 no. 4 128–37
– *Short Novels* ('To Have and to Lose,' 'Duishen,' and 'Mother-Earth') Moscow n.d.

- *Tales of the Mountains and Steppes* 2nd ed Moscow 1973
- *The White Ship* Tr Mirra Ginsburg. New York 1972
- *The White Steamship* Tr and with an Afterword by Tatyana and George Feifer. London 1972
Aitmatov, Chingiz, and Kaltai Mukhamedzhanov *The Ascent of Mount Fuji* Tr Nicholas Bethell. New York 1975
Bondarev, Iurii *The Hot Snow* Moscow 1976
- *The Last Shots* Moscow n.d.
- *Silence* Tr Elizaveta Fen. London 1965
Bykov, Vasil' *The Ordeal* London 1972
- *The Third Flare* Moscow 1963
- 'The Wolf Pack' *Soviet Literature* 1975 no. 5 15–115
Rasputin, Valentin 'Being Yourself' an interview with Evgenii Osetrov *Soviet Literature* 1977 no. 5 148–54
- 'French Lesson' *Soviet Literature* 1975 no. 1 165–86
- *Live and Remember* Tr Antonina W. Bouis. New York 1978
Trifonov, Iurii 'The Exchange' in *The Ardis Anthology of Recent Russian Literature* Ed Carl Proffer and Ellendea Proffer. Ann Arbor 1976 117–63
- *The Impatient Ones* Moscow 1978
- *The Long Goodbye* The novellas: 'The Exchange,' 'Taking Stock,' 'The Long Goodbye' Tr Helen P. Burlingame and Ellendea Proffer. Ann Arbor 1978
- *Students* Moscow 1953
Zalygin, Sergei 'By the Irtysh' (From the Chronicles of the Krutye Luki Village) *Soviet Literature* 1965 no. 7 3–94
- 'Salt Valley' (A Chapter from the Novel) *Soviet Literature* 1969 no. 5 51–124
- *The Commission* in *Soviet Literature* 1977 no. 1 3–101, no. 2 69–125, and no. 3 36–76
- 'Thoughts About My Profession' *Soviet Literature* 1966 no. 11 147–53

Index

Abramov, Fedor 16, 75; *Priasliny* (The Priaslins) 16

Aitmatov, Chingiz x, xi, xiii, 7, 31, 32–46, 74, 79; 'Belyi dozhd' ' (White Rain) 32; 'Belyi parokhod (Posle skazki)' (The White Steamship) xiii, 33, 35, 36, 37, 38, 39, 41, 42, 43, 101, 107; 'Dzhamilia' (Dzhamilia) 32, 33, 34; 'Litsom k litsu' (Face to Face) 32, 34, 79; 'Materinskoe pole' (Mother Earth) 34, 35, 40; 'Pegii pes, begushchii kraem moria' (Spotted Dog by the Sea's Edge) 33, 36, 41–3; 'Pervyi uchitel' ' (The First Teacher) 33, 34; *Povesti gor i stepei* (Tales of the Mountains and Steppes) 33; 'Proshchai, Gul'sary!' (Farewell, Gul'sary!) 33, 34, 35, 36, 37; 'Rannie zhuravli' (Early Cranes) 33, 36, 39, 40, 41; 'Soperniki' (Rivals) 32; 'Topolek moi v krasnoi kosynke' (To Have and to Lose) 33, 34, 35; 'Trudnaia pereprava' (The Difficult Crossing) 32; 'Verbliuzhii glaz' (A Camel's Eye) 33, 34; 'Voskhozhdenie na Fudziiamu' (The Ascent of Mount Fuji) 33, 43–4

Anan'ev, Anatolii 16, 18–19; *Gody bez voiny* (Years without War) 19

Arena Stage Theatre, Washington, DC 33

Astaf'ev, Viktor 16, 20–1, 30; 'Pastukh i pastushka' (The Shepherd and the Shepherdess) 20–1; *Poslednii poklon* (The Last Respects) 20; *Tsar'-ryba* (The King of the Fish) 21

Avyžius, Jonas 14–15; *Poteriannyi krov* (The Lost Shelter) 14–15

Babel', Isaak 99

Baklanov, Grigorii 24–5; *Druz'ia* (Friends) 24–5

Barabash, Iurii 8, 9, 11

Beliaeva, Liliia xii

Belov, Vasilii 16, 18, 75; 'Privychnoe delo' (That's How It Is) 18

Bitov, Andrei xiii

Blok, Aleksandr 5

Bocharov, A. 50, 102

Bocharov, Vadim 29

Bokarev, Gennadii 26–7; 'Stalevary' (The Steel Founders) 26–7, 30

Bondarev, Iurii x, xiii, 15, 31, 48, 54–60; *Bereg* (The Shore) xiii, 31, 57–9; *Goriachii sneg* (The Hot Snow) 56–7; *Tishina* (Silence) 55–6

Briusov, Valerii 5

Brown, Deming x; *Soviet Russian Literature Since Stalin* x

Bykov, Vasil' x, xiii, 16, 31, 48, 49–54, 59–60; 'Alpiiskaia ballada' (Alpine Ballad) 51; 'Ataka s khodu' (Full Speed At-